DESIGNING WITH BLACK

Architecture & Interiors

DESIGNING WITH BLACK

Architecture & Interiors

STEPHEN CRAFTI

images
Publishing

Acknowledgements

I would like to thank all the architects featured in this book, as well as the
many photographers who have contributed to making this book so special.

I would particularly like to thank my partner Naomi, for her incredible
support, constructive comments and, of course, her love of all things black.

Stephen Crafti

Published in Australia in 2013 by
The Images Publishing Group Pty Ltd
ABN 89 059 734 431
6 Bastow Place, Mulgrave, Victoria 3170, Australia
Tel: +61 3 9561 5544 Fax: +61 3 9561 4860
books@imagespublishing.com
www.imagespublishing.com

Copyright © The Images Publishing Group Pty Ltd 2013
The Images Publishing Group Reference Number: 1053

All rights reserved. Apart from any fair dealing for the purposes
of private study, research, criticism or review as permitted under
the Copyright Act, no part of this publication may be reproduced,
stored in a retrieval system or transmitted in any form by any means,
electronic, mechanical, photocopying, recording or otherwise,
without the written permission of the publisher.

National Library of Australia Cataloguing-in-Publication entry:
Author: Crafti, Stephen
Title: Designing with black : architecture & interiors/
                 Stephen Crafti
ISBN: 9781864704853 (hbk.)
Subjects: Black
                 Architecture, domestic
                 Interior decoration
                 Black in art
Dewey number   700.1

Edited by Driss Fatih

Designed by The Graphic Image Studio Pty Ltd, Mulgrave, Australia
www.tgis.com.au

Pre-publishing services by United Graphic Pte Ltd, Singapore

Printed by Everbest Printing Co. Ltd., in Hong Kong/China
on 140 gsm Sun Woodfree paper

IMAGES has included on its website a page for special
notices in relation to this and our other publications.
Please visit www.imagespublishing.com.

CONTENTS

- **7**   Foreword by Stephen Crafti
- **9**   Introduction

20 Open House	**74** Shadow Land	**140** Night Wing
26 Black Art	**80** Rubber Walls	**146** Love Shack
32 Pitch Black	**86** High Gloss	**152** Ink Grained
38 Casa Negra	**92** Jet Plain	**158** Render Black
44 Coal Face	**98** Motor Home	**164** Dark Clad
50 Ever Green	**104** Black Sea	**170** Black Out
56 Red Hot	**110** Point of View	**176** Light & Shade
62 Long Black	**116** Stained Black	**182** Shades of Black
68 Style Noir	**122** Light Box	**188** Black & Blue
	128 Black Forest	**194** Night on the Tiles
	134 Shingle Style	**200** Back to Black
		206 Sheer Black
		212 Rammed Earth
		218 Top Hat

224   Index of Architects

Foreword

STEPHEN CRAFTI
MELBOURNE, AUSTRALIA

Black has always been my favourite colour – or absence of colour. If I was given a choice, I would live in a black house. It could be made of concrete, steel or even timber, as long as it was black. While I dream of one day of living in a black house, my recent move to an unrenovated home provided the opportunity for thinking black. ■ While the 1930s duplex (one up, one down) I purchased would look odd painted black, a renovation did allow me to apply a 'black paint brush' across many of the surfaces. The timber floors, for example, concealed by carpet for nearly 80 years, were polished in lacquered black. This not only provided a strong contrast to the chalk-white walls, but also allowed light to reflect from the high-gloss finish. After the floors came new curtains. Although there was a vast range of colours to select, a sheer black curtain swatch won the day. While appearing slightly 'gothic' to the street, these black curtains allow the unadorned 1930s window frames to appear recessive in the façade. ■ When it came to planning a garden, black resurfaced. The tired silver-grey timber fences needed painting and black seemed an obvious choice. Everything I planted in the garden, from the moss-white birch trees to the oak-leaf hydrangeas appeared sharper against the black background. One nursery I spoke to suggested black irises would make a wonderful statement in the garden. Another garden supplier suggested a black magnolia tree as a wonderful feature. When it came to buying mulch for the garden beds, I found I was drawn to the black mulch, something I hadn't seen before. My son, who started a vegetable patch, included beans – black ones of course – a penchant for black must be genetic! And when the outdoor furniture was being recovered, the designer suggested black to complement the white plastic tubular frames. How could I resist? ■ However, when my partner designated one of the spare bedrooms as a walk-in wardrobe, it became clear that a book on black design was in the wings. Her clothes come in every shade of black. The only alternative is a small collection of white shirts. Even most of her contemporary jewellery is black, as are her shoes, handbags, scarves and even socks. Like black clothes and accessories, which appear timeless and elegant, black houses appear ageless. Whether clad in stained black timber or in steel, designing with black makes a quiet statement among considerably 'noisier' neighbours. Black homes provide a quiet ambience in the streetscape, allowing the landscape to predominate. ■ Those with a penchant for black, be it in what they wear, the objects that surround them, or their 'outlook in life', will appreciate this journey through black homes. Like my own house, where black seems to camouflage any irregularities, black design helps to remove superfluous detail that takes away from the overall concept. And although I'm surrounded by black in my current home, there's a feeling of solidity, not despair.

Introduction

This book on black houses includes buildings that are entirely black. Other projects are best described as houses with 'black additions', allowing a new contemporary wing to appear recessive behind a period home. There are also black houses in this book which use a 'splash of white' to articulate a pathway or entrance. And although these homes are essentially black, the interiors are often white – partially or entirely – to provide a sharp contrast to the exterior. ■ Many of the homes featured in this book also bring a touch of black to the interior. This could take the form of stained black timber feature walls, stained black timber floors or even black laminate joinery for kitchens and bathrooms. Black furniture also features prominently, sometimes placed against white, such as dining tables. ■ While black designs have their converts, the effect is maximised only when they are placed in the right context. For example, one black house, featuring a black steel façade, was the perfect solution between two inner city homes. This contemporary house is not only recessive in the Victorian streetscape, but creates a sense of intrigue from the outset. Another house, clad in black zinc, does not overshadow its neighbours – significant homes built during the twentieth century. ■ Black is both a geographical and cultural phenomenon. Black houses, for example, are integral to the culture of New Zealand. The climate in New Zealand suits black houses, with the lush vegetation providing a wonderful framework. In contrast, cities such as Sydney are where the white house rules supreme – understandably, given the strength of the natural light. ■ Black can also camouflage any irregularities, and black design helps to remove superfluous detail that takes away from the overall concept.

The Ridge Road Residence by studiofour, clad entirely in white mahogany, stained black, appears like a burnt log in the landscape. ■ Photo: Shannon McGrath

This house, elevated on steel poles, is partially clad in black polycarbonate. "We obviously love black, but in this instance it was used to diffuse the light as well as screen a neighbouring home", says architect Andrew Simpson. To further diffuse the light, the architects created a secondary 'skin' of clear polycarbonate. A gap between these two layers purges hot air during the warmer months. The external black polycarbonate wall, which appears to wrap around the roof, also slightly twists. "We saw this form like the canvas awning you often see attached to caravans", says the architect. ■ Photo: Christine Francis

Minimalist black furniture and light fittings, set against pure white walls and floor, create a cool, restrained tone. The bathroom, which appears as a black cube in the space, is sharply defined against white floors. All joinery units, including the panelling around the bathroom, are clad in black anodised aluminium. The black-and-white theme was also the result of the owner's brief for a tranquil space to which she could retreat. "She didn't want to be distracted by colour in the house", says architect Ian Moore. ■ Photo: Iain D. MacKenzie

Black stained timber was used for the library and floor of this house by Nixon Tulloch Fortey. ■ Photo: Shannon McGrath; works of art by Peter Booth, Sam Leach, Nick Mangan, Linda Marrinon, David Noonan, Wendy Stavrianos and Tony Tuckson

In the formal dining room of this house by Nixon Tulloch Fortey, the walls are painted a dark charcoal black to accentuate the art. "We selected quite a graphic palette", says George Fortey, pointing out the black bentwood timber chairs combined with a white dining table. ■ Photo: Shannon McGrath; painting by Daniel Boyd

Nixon Tulloch Fortey Architecture used black to great effect in this interior. European oak floors stained black continue from the kitchen and living areas up the staircase, and contrast sharply with the pure white walls. The art on the landing is an arresting combination of both.
■ Photo: Shannon McGrath; painting by David Griggs

The tallowwood used for joinery, columns, beams and cladding appears considerably richer when juxtaposed against black stained timber. The combination of the two coloured timbers also creates a strong graphic quality, with architectural details highlighted. "We used fairly restrained materials", says architect Tai Ropiha of Choi Ropiha Fighera, pointing out the polished concrete floors. "This helps to create that sense of calm our clients were looking for", he adds. ■ Photo: Simon Whitbread Photography

"We stained the walls along the passage black to further link the interior to the outdoors", says Dave Strachan of Strachan Group Architects, of this house on Waiheke Island. "There's a long tradition of black houses in New Zealand. It comes from our landscape, recalling Ponga ferns with their black trunks and stems", he adds. ■ Photo: Patrick Reynolds

The geometry of the interior of this house is the result of the finely expressed black zinc roof. Constructed in black zinc, steel and glass, these dramatic pitches create the geometry for the interior of the home. Translucent glass windows provide light, as well as privacy. And to ensure maximum natural light, the triangular roof forms are orientated to the sunlight. "At night, the house literally glows like a lantern", says architect Tony Chenchow of Chenchow Little Architects. Equally striking are the dramatic black steel beams inside the home. Used for structural support, as well as being decorative, these black steel beams cleverly distort perspectives, as well as animating the spaces. ■ Photo: John Gollings

The owner of this house, designed by Joshua Zoeller, specifically requested a studio for his calligraphy painting. With a keen interest in Japan, Zoeller included a white pebbled Japanese-style garden outside the studio. ■ Photo: Andrew Shepherd

OPEN

CHOI ROPIHA FIGHERA

This lot was once occupied by a 1960s house. While the two-storey cream brick building was structurally sound, it had a mundane and suburban feel. "Our clients wanted to come home to an oasis every night, something that felt quite protected", says architect Tai Ropiha, co-director of Choi Ropiha Fighera. ■ Rather than compromise with the existing structure, Choi Ropiha Fighera designed a new house. Clad in cypress, stained black, and golden-coloured tallowwood, the two-storey house leaves the suburban street behind. A long pathway on the side of the house leads to an internal courtyard. "The words 'calm and tranquil' were included in our client's brief. Black tends to add to the sense of tranquility", says Ropiha. ■ The public spaces in the house are grouped around the courtyard, creating a sense of fluidity, as well as framing the swimming pool. An open-plan kitchen and living areas extend across the entire width of the house. Featuring large timber and glass stackable doors, the house can be completely opened up. "The children use the deck as another room", says Ropiha, who elevated the house 1.2 metres above ground level. "The area is expected to flood once every one hundred years", he adds. ■ The tallowwood, used for joinery, columns, beams and cladding, appears considerably richer when juxtaposed against the black stained timber. The combination of the two coloured timbers also creates a strong graphic quality, with architectural details highlighted. "We've used fairly restrained materials", says Ropiha, pointing out the polished concrete floors. "This helps to create that sense of calm our clients were looking for", he adds. ■ Although the three bedrooms on the first floor, including the main, are enclosed, Choi Ropiha Fighera loosened the 'edges' where possible. The children's bedrooms, for example, feature large sliding doors, almost the size of an entire wall. These allow the bedrooms to connect to a built-in study, which forms part of the passage. ■ There's a sense of drama once past the front gate. "We've created a series of thresholds that remove you from suburbia. And staining the timber black just intensifies that experience", adds Ropiha. ■ PHOTOGRAPHY: SIMON WHITBREAD PHOTOGRAPHY

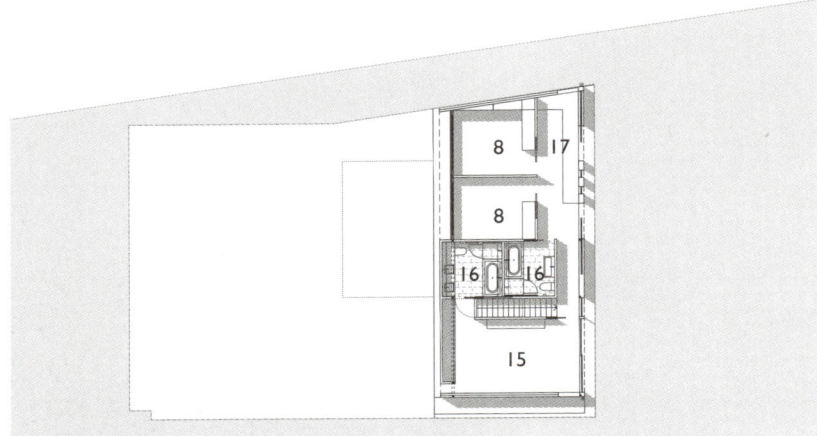

FIRST FLOOR

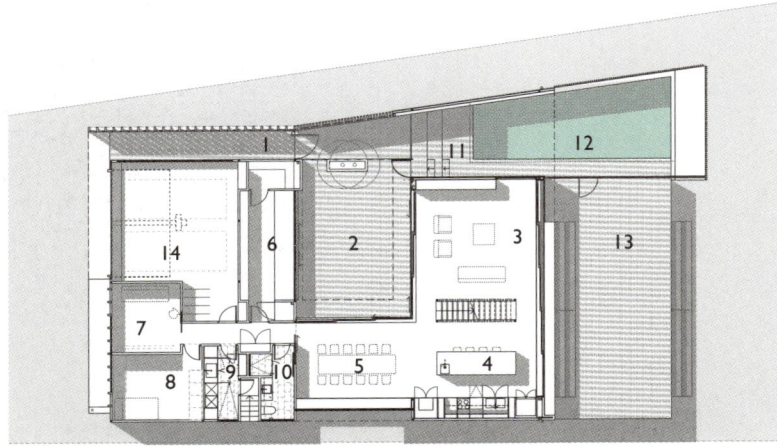

GROUND FLOOR

1 Entry
2 Courtyard
3 Living
4 Kitchen
5 Dining
6 Office
7 Media room
8 Bedroom
9 Laundry
10 Shower
11 Outdoor room
12 Pool
13 Deck
14 Garage
15 Master bedroom
16 Ensuite
17 Study

BLACK

IAN MOORE ARCHITECTS

ArT

Originally built in 1895 as a grocery warehouse, this modest building on an 84-square-metre site is now a striking contemporary inner-city home. Designed by architect Ian Moore, the warehouse-style home is a composition of black and white. "We made the decision that everything added was in black, while anything original was left white", says Moore. ■ However, before the areas were colour-coded, Moore removed many of the features added by the previous owner – an artist – who was using the warehouse as both home and studio. Recycled windows and French doors were taken away. Replacing these are steel-framed windows and doors, in black. "I've always enjoyed working with black steel. But steel seemed an appropriate material, given its thickness (10mm) and the limited space available (150 square metres internally)", says Moore. ■ The black-and-white theme was also the result of the owner's brief for a tranquil space to which she could retreat. Moore's client also wanted him to provide an appropriate backdrop for her extensive collection of black-and-white photos collected from around the world. "She didn't want to be distracted by colour in the house", says Moore. ■ At ground level are the garage, kitchen, dining and living areas. A flight of stairs, clad in black rubber and framed by black steel walls, leads to the study, bathroom and main bedroom. The bathroom, which appears as a black cube in the space, is sharply defined against white floors. All joinery units, including the panelling around the bathroom, are clad in black anodised aluminium. The bookcase in the living room is made entirely from 10mm-thick black steel. The desk and coffee table are made from two sheets of glass – one black and one white – bonded together to form a total thickness of 10mm, which matches the thickness of the 10mm-thick black steel used throughout the warehouse. ■ Fortunately, Moore's client came to the house with primarily black furniture. What wasn't black – two Art Deco armchairs from Paris – were re-upholstered in black fabric. "It was fortuitous that her mirrored dressing table had stained black timber legs", says Moore. ■ While colour dates many homes, be they renovated in the 1950s, 1970s or more recently, this home appears timeless with its restricted colour palette. "The way we've used black is also about telling a story and letting people know that black is new – it's something we've clearly added", says Moore. ■ PHOTOGRAPHY: IAIN D. MACKENZIE

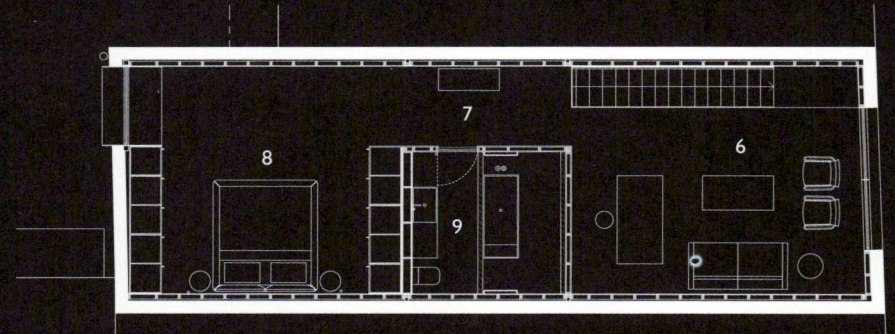

FIRST FLOOR

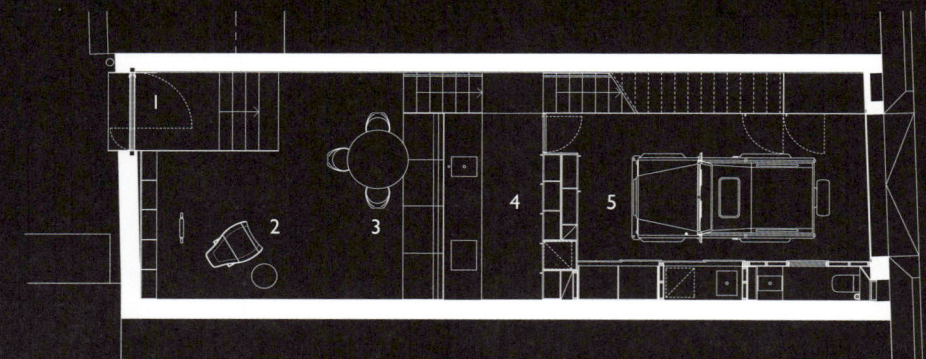

GROUND FLOOR

1 Entry
2 Living
3 Dining
4 Kitchen
5 Garage
6 Study
7 Gallery
8 Bedroom
9 Ensuite

PITCH

This black house by Chenchow Little Architects is often referred to by the architects as 'gem-like' in form. But instead of curved crater-like surfaces, the geometry of the interior is the result of the finely expressed black zinc roof. Constructed in black zinc, steel and glass, the house sits on an escarpment overlooking Sydney Harbour. ■ When a local authority edict was issued stating that every roof in the area had to be pitched, Chenchow Little literally took them at their word. But rather than one traditional pitched roof, this house is almost a 'symphony of black pitches', with roof angles skewed in different directions. "As the house is on an escarpment, Council didn't want houses above to look onto a flat roof", says architect Tony Chenchow. "The black steel makes the forms more recessive in the landscape, as do the exterior black steel louvres", says Chenchow, who works closely with his life and business partner, Stephanie Little. ■ These dramatic pitches create the geometry for the interior of the home. Translucent glass windows, also angular, provide light, as well as privacy. And to ensure maximum natural light, the triangular roof forms are orientated to the sunlight. "At night, the house literally glows like a lantern", says Chenchow. Equally striking are the dramatic black steel beams inside the home. Used for structural support, as well as being decorative, these black steel beams cleverly distort perspectives, as well as animating the spaces. ■ The glazed façade is leveraged to the harbour. The architects allow slivers of light to enter by means of an open-roofed L-shaped courtyard, separating the kitchen from the lounge. "We've tried to keep the living spaces as open as possible to allow the form to be read from several vantage points. The black steel beams certainly articulate the volumes", says Chenchow. ■ As the faceted ceilings and angular windows caused the senses to go into overdrive, the architects used a restrained palette of materials, including fibro cement sheets for walls and a neutral palette for areas such as the kitchen. The kitchen, for example, features a long Corian bench. "Our clients were keen for us to use limited materials", says Chenchow. ■ Chenchow Little Architects set themselves an enormous task when they decided to 'play with the traditional pitch'. Combining triangular shapes with a rectilinear floor plan may have caused some sleepless nights. "Resolving this geometry does take time. Everything had to be considered to the nth degree, whether it was the placement of doors or joinery", says Chenchow. ■ PHOTOGRAPHY: JOHN GOLLINGS

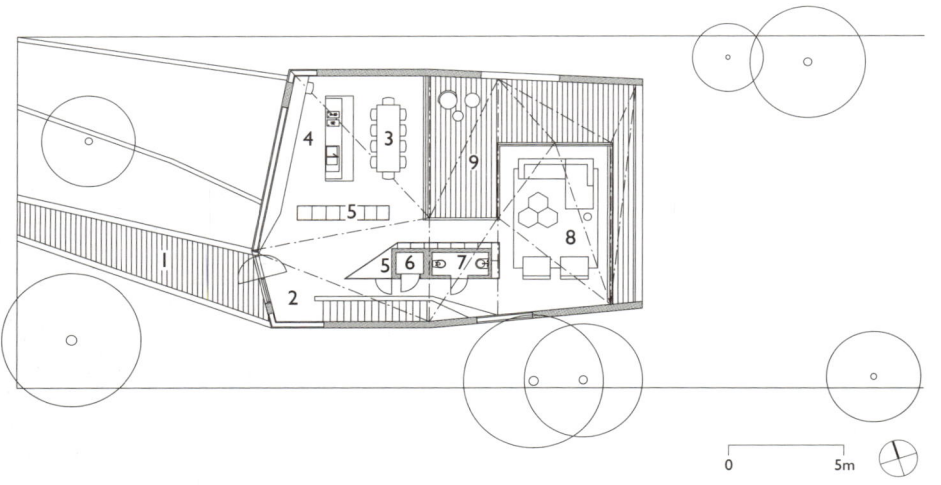

0 5m

1 Entry bridge
2 Entry
3 Dining
4 Kitchen
5 Store
6 Lift
7 Powder room
8 Living
9 Deck

CASA

REMY ARQUITECTOS

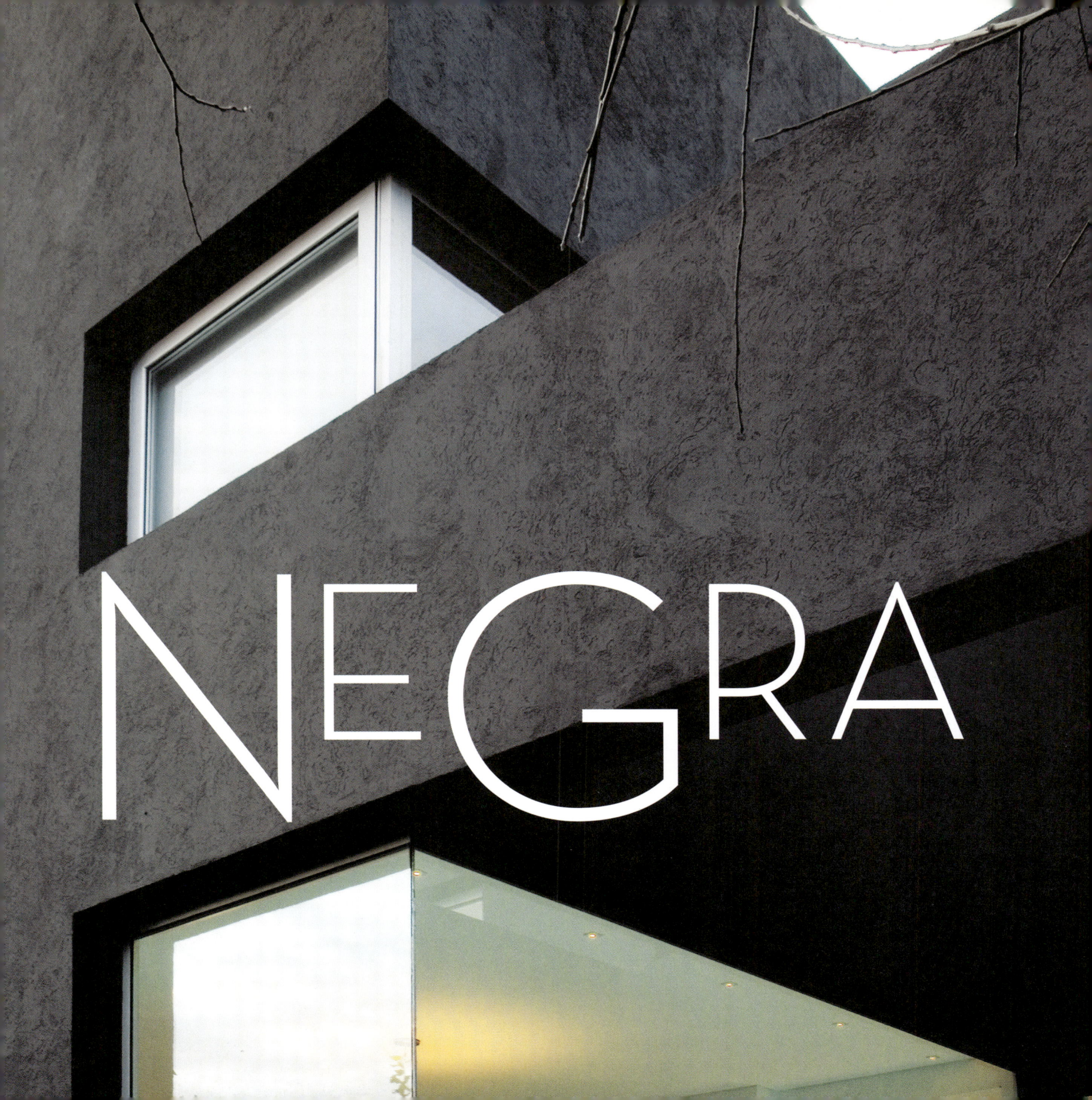

Designed by Remy Arquitectos, this black house is located 40 kilometres from Buenos Aires. Part of a gated community, there was initial resistance to a black house, when most of the adjacent homes were either white or grey. "Many of the residents saw a black house as a negative, but after several discussions they thought the idea was acceptable", says architect Andres Remy, director of the practice. ■ The two-storey house, of rendered brick and painted entirely black, appears relatively restrained, from the street. There are a couple of small windows on the front façade, as well as a high brick wall, also painted black. "Our clients were more concerned about the layout of rooms, with the public areas at ground level, and the private areas on the first floor. They were quite open as to the design, as well as the colour", says Remy. ■ At ground level the formal living areas are at the front of the house. And separated by a 'bridge' at the rear of the house, overlooking a lake, are the kitchen and living areas. Water surrounds these rooms, extending to the outdoors in the form of a swimming pool. One of the most striking features of the house is the cantilevered main bedroom wing, extending 3 metres in length. This animates the rear façade as well as providing sun protection for the outdoor areas. ■ In contrast to the all-black exterior, the home's interior is all white. White porcelain tiles feature on the floors, and the ceilings and walls are pristine white. To extend the white ceilings, the architects also painted the undercroft of the cantilevered main bedroom white. "We wanted to create a sense of continuity with the outdoors. The white undercroft allows the interior spaces to feel larger as a result", says Remy. The only colour used in the house is a vivid red wall functioning as a balustrade to the staircase linking the two levels. "It's a minimal colour palette, deliberately chosen to accentuate the view of the lake", adds Remy. ■ PHOTOGRAPHY: ALEJANDRO PERAL

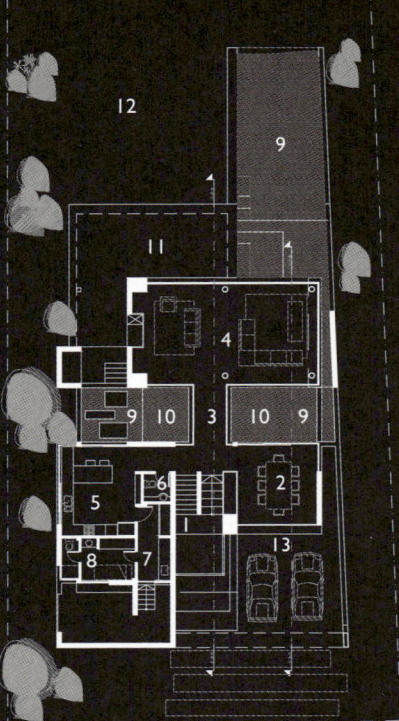

GROUND FLOOR

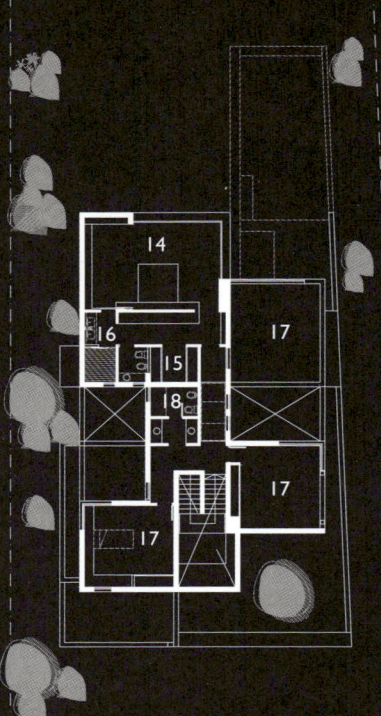

FIRST FLOOR

8 Maid's quarters
9 Pool
10 Void
11 Terrace
12 Garden
13 Garage
14 Master bedroom
15 Dressing room
16 Ensuite
17 Bedroom
18 Bathroom

COAL

MUIR MENDES

FACE

Architects often wear head-to-toe black. And like architects Bruno Mendes and Amy Muir, they also sometimes live in a black house. "Black houses don't generally scream for attention, being recessive in both urban and rural settings", says Muir, who designed her house with life and business partner Mendes. ■ The Muir Mendes house, in Melbourne's inner city, sits quietly in a narrow one-way street. Wedged between a Victorian worker's cottage and a two-storey 1980s brick townhouse, the house features an all-black painted steel façade. The steel front door is also painted black, along with what's referred to as a 'drawbridge' style front window that allows a sliver of light to enter the front bedroom. "We wanted to create a 'blank' façade, something that would speak to both neighbouring homes, of different styles", says Mendes. ■ Beyond the black façade is a predominantly white interior. White walls feature in the open-plan kitchen and living areas, as well as in the two bedrooms. However, to accentuate the white walls and timber floors, there are strong accents of black and charcoal. Charcoal-black felt Echo Panels, for example, frame the passage to the living areas. These irregular-shaped panels also appear in the kitchen joinery, partially located under a black folded steel staircase. "The Echo Panels are like the black cross-section you see on architects' plans", says Muir, who was keen to exaggerate the folded ceiling in the living areas. ■ The black theme of the Muir Mendes house also extends to some of the built-in furniture, also designed by the couple. As well as the striking black steel stairs, there's a built-in steel desk for the first-floor study. Black steel was also used to conceal the heating units. The bookshelves are also made from black steel. And to add drama to the interior, as well as protection from the harsh sunlight, the architects included an army fatigue net as a sunshade over the central skylight, evocative of burnt leaves. ■ While the home's black façade 'fades' in the street, the interior, with its white walls, is highly graphic. "We wanted the black façade to have the opposite effect to the interior. The white walls in the passage appear even more brilliant when you first walk in", adds Muir. ■ PHOTOGRAPHY: PETER BENNETTS

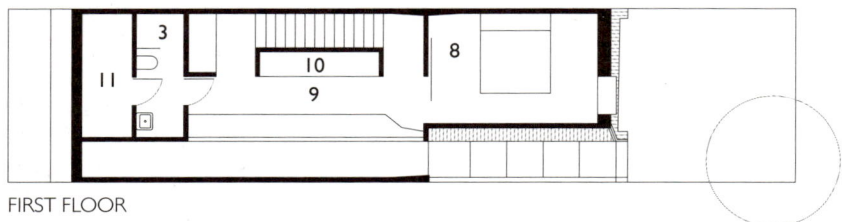
FIRST FLOOR

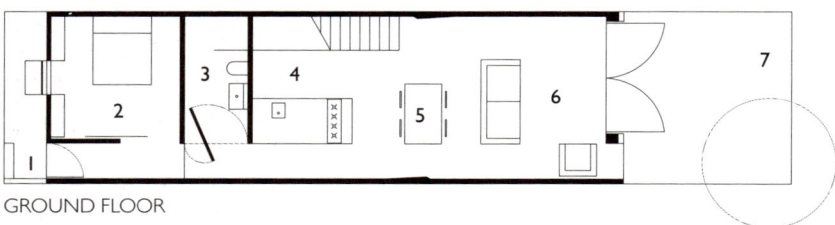
GROUND FLOOR

1 Entry
2 Bedroom
3 Bathroom
4 Kitchen
5 Dining room
6 Living room
7 Deck
8 Master bedroom
9 Study
10 Robe
11 Storage

EVER

MARC DIXON ARCHITECT

This single-storey interwar house (circa 1940s) was in almost original condition when architect Marc Dixon first inspected it. The brick house featured a lean-to, as well as a sleep-out and outside toilet. "My clients needed another bedroom. They also wanted an inside toilet", says Dixon, who was mindful of not detracting from the period home. "It's quite beautiful, even though some of the amenities were quite basic", he adds. ■ Dixon removed the lean-to, as well as the outdoor toilet. He replaced these with a striking contemporary wing, constructed in black steel with a punchy lime-green door and window trims. "The owner was more concerned about the amount of light entering the house, rather than what colour cladding would be used", says Dixon, who included a 'pop-up' void above the kitchen's central island bench. ■ The contemporary wing includes an open-plan kitchen and dining area. And upstairs there's a child's bedroom and bathroom. Dixon retained the original sleep-out, which is now used as a study. The black steel is a contrast to the heavier brick masonry of the original home. Black steel also ensures the two-storey addition can't be easily detected from the street, which is essentially intact with similar period homes. ■ While there are bolts of colour used for the home's exterior, including a mint-green steel door, the majority of colour appears on the interior. There's bright red-backed glass above the kitchen bench, complementing the lime-green window and door trims. And the bathrooms feature a riot of coloured tiles. Other materials, such as the timber underside of the upstairs bedroom, also provide a striking contrast to the black palette. ■ One area where black wasn't considered was the steel roof over the new wing. Dixon used bands of yellow and brown hues. "A black steel roof would have absorbed all the heat. These lighter colours are more reflective", says Dixon, who is also conscious of using colours appropriate to the home's orientation. "You want to avoid using black if the orientation receives full afternoon sunlight", he adds. ■ PHOTOGRAPHY: KEVIN HUI

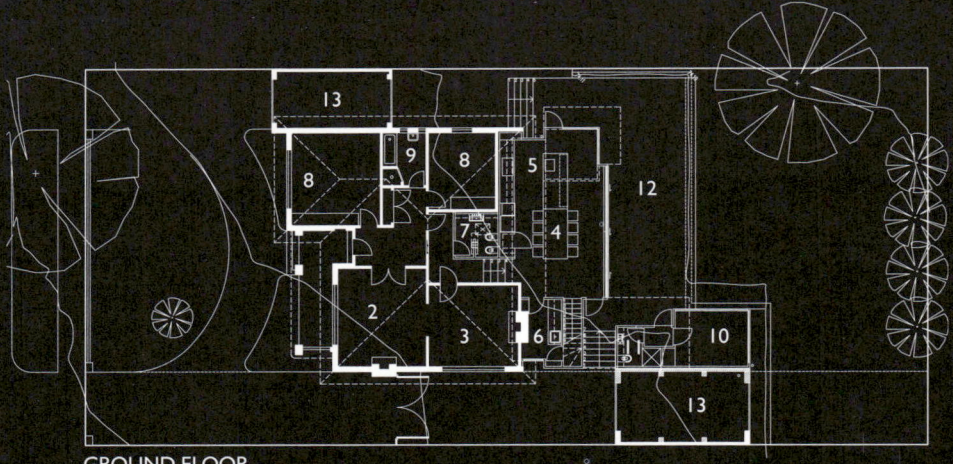

GROUND FLOOR

1 Entry
2 Lounge
3 Formal dining room
4 Dining
5 Kitchen
6 Laundry
7 Powder room
8 Bedroom
9 Bathroom
10 Guest bedroom
11 Ensuite
12 Deck
13 Garage

ReD

BELLEMO & CAT

This black steel house appears like a black tent from the distance. However, as one approaches the structure, it's clear that this modest home is a solid structure. Designed by Bellemo & Cat architects, the form, as well as the colour of the steel, was inspired by the owner's ethnic heritage. ■ As the owner comes from a Middle Eastern background, the idea for a Bedouin-inspired house emerged. Perched on the top of a hill, the home's black silhouette even includes a tent-like flap adjacent to the front door. "We wanted to protect the entrance from the wind. But we also wanted to define the point of entry", says architect Michael Bellemo, who worked closely with his life and business partner, artist Cat Mcleod, on this project. ■ At approximately 85 square metres, the house is essentially one large room. The kitchen, living and dining areas form the main space. There is also a separate bedroom and bathroom. And to provide for additional accommodation, there's a roll-out bed in the main living area. ■ While the home's exterior is completely black, with the exception of a fibro cement panel painted red, the interior is mostly red, including the ceilings and walls. Even the kitchen joinery, extending along one side of the space, is made from red laminate. The red walls and joinery are accentuated by a black stained timber plywood floor. To frame the views, as well as provide cross-ventilation, the architects inserted a long slot window on one side of the house. ■ While the house appears quite sombre from the initial sighting, it presents a completely different side once you pass the front door, with the vibrant red interior being more pronounced as a result of the contrast. ■

PHOTOGRAPHY: SONIA MANGIAPANE

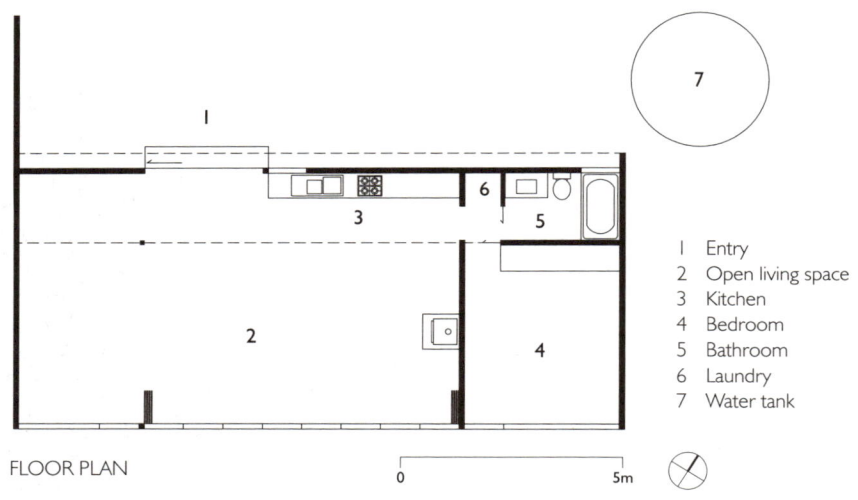

FLOOR PLAN 0 5m

1 Entry
2 Open living space
3 Kitchen
4 Bedroom
5 Bathroom
6 Laundry
7 Water tank

LONG

INTERMODE

BLACK

Nick Carr, the name behind Intermode, has designed several black homes. "Black is simply a great colour. It allows a house to sit subtly in the landscape. Black is perfect for regional settings", says Carr, who was commissioned to design this house by a graphic designer. "We tend to attract clients who share our aesthetic, and of course a love for black", he adds. ■ Located in Emerald, an hour's drive east of Melbourne, this black house is on an elevated site, overlooking the Warburton Ranges. Originally the owner went to another architect who presented him with plans for a two-storey house. Unfortunately thier budget didn't allow for this, so they proceeded with a rectilinear single-storey home that met all of their needs and design aspirations, but kept them within budget. ■ Intermode excavated the steep site, the point of arrival being a black steel roof and a black wall. "If we didn't use a black steel roof, you'd notice the form of the roof on arrival, rather than these spectacular ranges. We also didn't want the roof to reflect light", says Carr. Finished in shadowclad timber, stained black, the Emerald house features generous glazing on three sides with black powder-coated window frames. Even the fascia of the house is black, with the undercroft being white. ■ To achieve the brief within budget, the house features a main bedroom at one end, and two smaller bedrooms at the other. While there's an open-plan kitchen and living and dining areas separating these bedrooms, there's also a large home office. "Our client wanted the option of being able to occasionally work from home", says Carr. ■ In contrast to the black exterior, the interior, apart from black stained timber floors, is all white. As well as painted white walls, the kitchen joinery is white laminate with stone benches. With all the walls painted white, the black window and doorframes become more pronounced. "You're particularly aware of these black mullions as you move along the main passage", says Carr. ■ While the black house accentuates the mountain ranges in the distance, it also intensifies the lush bush setting. Silver birch trees, framing one corner of the house, also stand out against the black palette. "It's a 'clean' palette and appeals to clients with a strong design aesthetic", adds Carr. ■ PHOTOGRAPHY: MICHAEL WEARNE

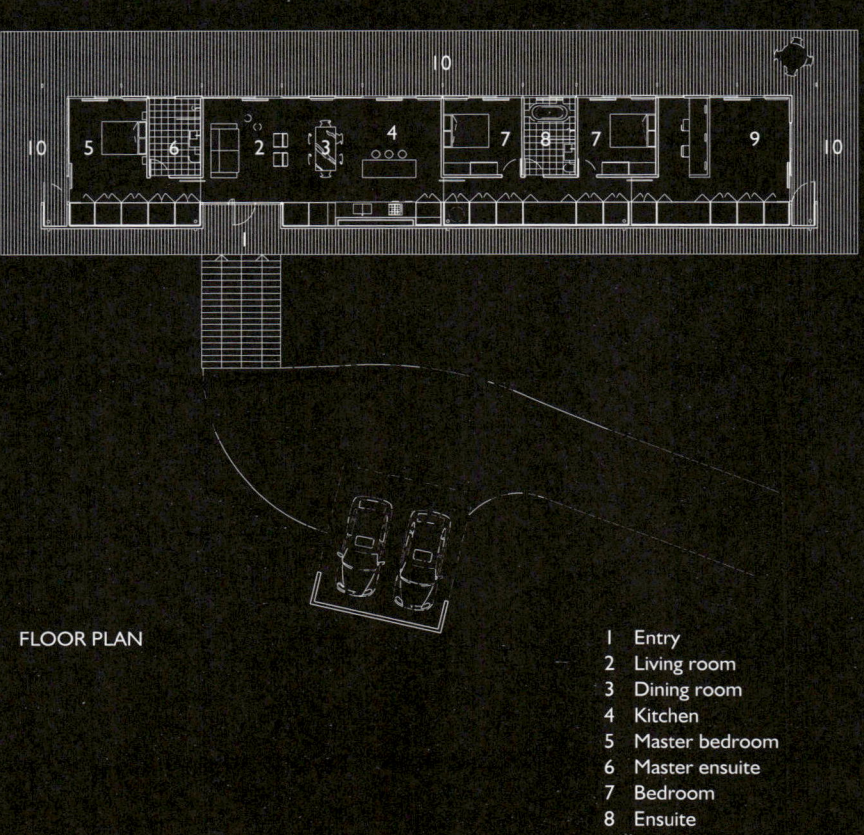

FLOOR PLAN

1 Entry
2 Living room
3 Dining room
4 Kitchen
5 Master bedroom
6 Master ensuite
7 Bedroom
8 Ensuite
9 Study
10 Deck

StYLe

FABRE/deMARIEN

Designed by Fabre/deMarien architecture, this big black house in Bordeaux, France, has the feel of a warehouse. Entrance to the home is via a steel mesh garage door, with little indication of the house beyond. The place was originally a garage. ■ Spread over two levels, the house is designed around a courtyard. At ground level are the bedrooms, while the first floor is given over to the living areas, including a protected outdoor terrace (covered by a shade cloth). "The façades of the building function like a double skin, the external layer being an insulated metal sandwich panel, with the internal layer finished by the steel cladding panels", says architect Julie Fabre, co-director of the practice, who worked closely with fellow director and architect Matthieu de Marien. ■ As well as black steel walls, the interior is detailed in lacquered black steel, including staircases, railings and joinery such as the aluminium door- and window frames. Black steel mesh balustrades on the staircase are also used for dramatic effect. Even the polished concrete floors are tinted black, to provide a contrast to the internal white or neutral partitioned walls. The white walls, as well as the white joinery in the kitchen, create a sharp edge when set against the black floors, expressed steel beams and galvanized steel panels in the ceiling. The shade cloth on the first-floor terrace is also black. "Black is a strong colour without being overbearing. We see the black cladding like 'the little black dress' – chic and minimalist, in keeping with a modern industrial aesthetic", says de Marien, who was also mindful of the neighbourhood, where many homes are carved from local stone. ■ Fabre/deMarien also approved of their client's choice of furniture, which is predominantly black. And to intensify the mood, many of the owner's artworks are also black. "Black really suited the client's brief. But black also provides a wonderful backdrop for the vines and creepers which are left to colonise the external metal structures, staircases and boundary walls", says Fabre. ■ PHOTOGRAPHY: STEPHANE CHALMEAU

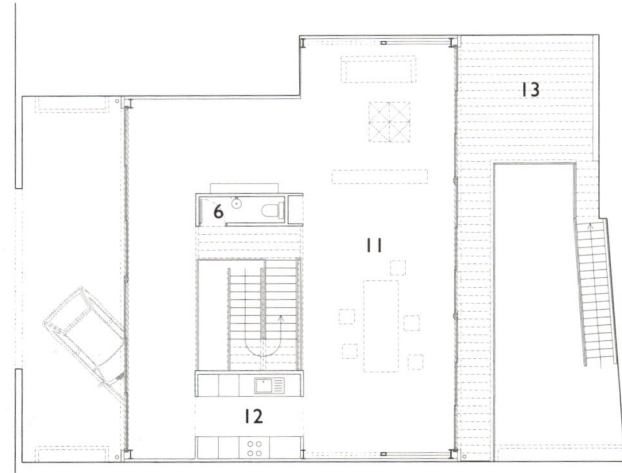

FIRST FLOOR

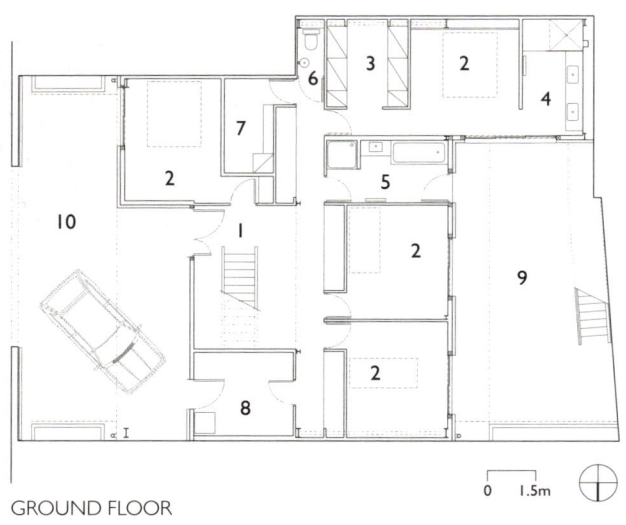

GROUND FLOOR

0 1.5m

1 Entry
2 Bedroom
3 Walk-in wardrobe
4 Ensuite
5 Bathroom
6 Powder room
7 Laundry
8 Store
9 Courtyard
10 Garage
11 Living
12 Kitchen
13 Terrace

SHADOW

TERROIR

This house, on the edge of Hobart, occupies one of the last bush blocks. Overlooking the city, and framed by established eucalypts, this house recedes in the landscape. "When we first inspected this site, the first thing we noticed were the deep shadows formed by the trees", says architect Scott Balmforth, a director of Terroir. ■ While many of the surrounding homes 'scream for attention', this house is deliberately understated. Appearing single-storey from the street, due to the slope of the land, the house is predominantly made from rendered cement, painted black and galvanised steel for some of the exterior walls and roof. Terroir also included tinted glass in the house, as well as black aluminium frames for windows and doors. "With most of the building 'blackened', the silvery grey steel roof becomes the focus. "The roof is more like an object", says Balmforth. ■ As the house slopes away from the street, the architects were able to include a level below ground. As well as a garage, there's a general purpose/rumpus room. In contrast to the dark exterior, the entrance to the first floor is stark. White walls frame a concrete staircase and generous light is brought into the interior from a skylight. To accentuate this light, Terroir included red stained plywood on one of the walls, emphasising the brilliant effect from the shafts of sunlight. ■ On the first floor of the house are three bedrooms, as well as the open-plan kitchen and living areas. While there's a dining and lounge area, there are also a variety of lounging nooks, including a study area. And like the home's exterior, the kitchen is recessive. Stained black timber walls enclose the kitchen, including a bulkhead. "We wanted to place greater emphasis on the view, rather than making the kitchen the home's focal point", says Balmforth. To heighten the effect of the surrounding trees, the architects also stained the plywood floors gloss black, reflecting the light, as well as intensifying the outlook. ■ Unlike many homes in the bush, this house sits in the shadows of the trees. "Like the owners, we're pleased this house isn't a feature of this hilltop. You really only notice this place when you walk up the stairs and see where you are", adds Balmforth. ■ PHOTOGRAPHY: SHANNON McGRATH AND RAY JOYCE

GROUND FLOOR

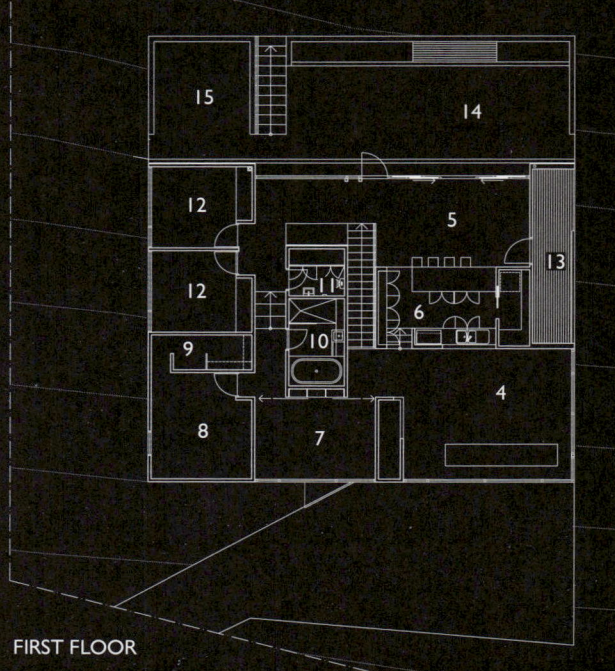
FIRST FLOOR

1 Entry
2 Store
3 Garage
4 Living room
5 Dining room
6 Kitchen
7 Study
8 Master bedroom
9 Walk-in wardrobe
10 Bathroom
11 Water closet
12 Bedroom
13 Deck
14 Courtyard
15 Service courtyard

RuBbeR

ANDREW SIMPSON ARCHITECTS

Designed by architects Andrew Simpson, Owen West and Steve Hatzellis, this house, known as the 'Scape House', isn't visible from the road. In fact, access to this weekend home is via a long winding dirt road. As one approaches the end of the 4-kilometre road, the ocean reveals itself, as does this unusual black house. "We saw the house as almost an object, like the granite boulders edging the property", says Simpson. ■ Designed for a couple with grown-up children, the house is located on disused farmland. "It's a fairly exposed site, with 270-degree views of the ocean", says Simpson. The brief from the owners was not only to capture these views from within the home, but also to have a weekender that was robust and low-maintenance. "Our clients also wanted something that was as comfortable for large groups of people, as it would be for themselves as a couple", says Simpson. ■ The form of the house, irregular in shape, started with the roof form, half skillion-shaped and half a more traditional pitch. And while tiles may be fine for a suburban house, the architects were keen to capture something of the beach culture. A black rubber membrane attached to plywood is evocative of surfers. "We used the rubber on the walls and roof to create one continuous form", says Simpson. The only contrast to the black is at the point of entry, which features white painted compressed cement sheet walls that continue to the interior. Black steel beams inside the house, set against white walls, also enliven the relatively neutral scheme. ■ One of the challenges for the architects was 'taming' the Roaring Forties, a wind system that makes sitting outside uncomfortable at certain times of the year. Their solution was to create an internalised 'verandah'. This not only frames views of the ocean, but also separates the sleeping areas from the living areas. And in keeping with the owner's brief for flexible accommodation, the verandah also functions as an additional sleeping area for family and friends. "People tend to be far more relaxed when they go on holidays. They don't necessarily expect ensuite bathrooms with every bedroom", says Simpson. ■ Against the ocean backdrop and sky, this house appears as a dark silhouette. "The form, as well as using black, creates an almost scale-less building. It almost 'morphs' depending on where you stand", says Simpson. ■ PHOTOGRAPHY: CHRISTINE FRANCIS

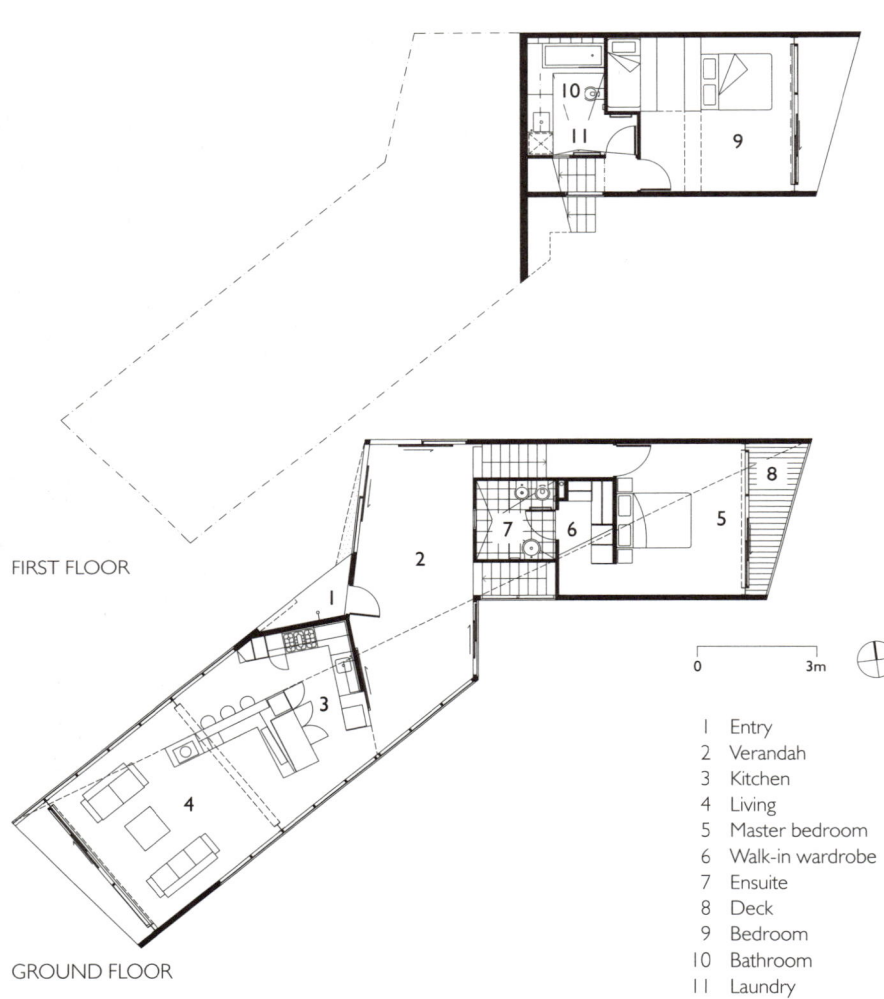

FIRST FLOOR

GROUND FLOOR

0   3m

1   Entry
2   Verandah
3   Kitchen
4   Living
5   Master bedroom
6   Walk-in wardrobe
7   Ensuite
8   Deck
9   Bedroom
10 Bathroom
11 Laundry

84

HIGH

b.e ARCHITECTURE

Located on Victoria's coastline, this cluster of black buildings could be a small village. However, these elevated homes, finished in a high-gloss black timber, are in fact one beach house. Elevated above a sprawling site, b.e architecture was keen to create a couple of low-rise pavilions rather than a house that dominated the area. Featuring pitched steel roofs, these pavilions are evocative of more traditional architectural styles. "We didn't think it was appropriate to design an angular all-white form in this pristine setting. The black timber forms are recessive to these gum trees", says architect Andrew Piva, director of the practice. ■ As the site slopes approximately 15 degrees, the architects were able to locate the garage and guest wing, comprising two bedrooms, bathrooms and kitchenette below the first floor living areas. And to anchor the building to the slope, the architects created a podium from chiselled stone boulders sourced from Malta. "These blocks are quite rough. They remind me of the early settler homes along the coast. They're also a contrast to the high-gloss black timber", says Piva. ■ The house is reached via a meandering pathway that leads to the front door. And rather than a lobby, the approach is directly into an open-plan kitchen and living areas. The kitchen, with a stone-finished island bench and stained oak joinery, is as informal as the living areas. ■ While the fireplace in the lounge is a focal point during the colder months, panoramic views of the ocean across the terrace are a 'permanent feature'. And to ensure these views are enjoyed from both inside and out, the architect included a large terrace with a covered pergola, to maximise its use. ■ The second pavilion on the site, also clad in black timber, is accessed via an enclosed walkway. This pavilion comprises three bedrooms, including the main bedroom, as well as bathrooms and dressing areas. And as there's a fall across the site, the architect was able to create a gulley-like effect linking the two pavilions. "We wanted to establish a strong relationship to the landscape, whether from the living areas or from bedrooms. But from all angles, we wanted the house to be recessive to the landscape. And we could achieve this by cladding the house in black timber", adds Piva. ■ PHOTOGRAPHY: PETER CLARKE

1	Entry
2	Living
3	Dining
4	Kitchen
5	Pantry
6	Rumpus room
7	Covered walkway
8	Master bedroom
9	Walk-in wardrobe
10	Ensuite
11	Bedroom
12	Powder room
13	Bathroom
14	Study
15	Linen
16	Laundry
17	Entertaining terrace
18	Covered terrace

GROUND FLOOR

JeT

BOWER ARCHITECTURE

The owners of this house had lived in the same property for many years, where they raised their children, now living elsewhere. And while they were happy to remain where they were, they were tired of living in the original home, a dark two-storey cream brick house. "Our clients had lived in the house for a long time. It wasn't the size of the home that concerned them, but the darkness, with small pokey rooms", says architect Jade Vidal, co-director of Bower Architecture. ■ Rather than try and remodel the original house for a couple who regularly have children and grandchildren visiting and staying over, the brief was for a new two-storey house. "Our clients wanted a house that was large, but also flexible", says Vidal. ■ Bower Architecture designed a two-storey house zoned around a central gallery, clad in black zinc and charcoal concrete blocks. The black 'pop-out' zinc-clad façade, which contains a rumpus room for the grandchildren, hovers above a black painted garage door. Even the steel window frames are black. One of the few non-black elements in the façade is the sliver of timber cladding above the home's entrance. "We wanted to direct people to the front door", says Vidal. ■ Inside the house, the colour palette is almost all white. White walls, as well as a polished plaster wall in the living area, reflect light from highlight windows. The only black features inside the house are pendant lights above the dining table. "We wanted the interior to be a strong contrast from the exterior and be flooded with natural light and a sense of warmth," says Vidal, who was conscious of a neighbouring two-storey house restricting the natural light. ■ Bower chose a black palette for the exterior, in particular black zinc, for several reasons. The street in which the house is located includes a variety of architectural styles built over the course of the 20th century. "We didn't want this house to dominate the other houses, but we also wanted to design something that was strong and contemporary, not derivative of other styles. The black colours also allow the scale of the house to recede into the streetscape", says Vidal. The architects were also attracted to zinc, primarily due to its malleability and durability. "Zinc has a certain softness, and it's not shiny like a lot of other materials. This makes it ideal for residential projects", adds Vidal. ■ PHOTOGRAPHY: SHANNON McGRATH

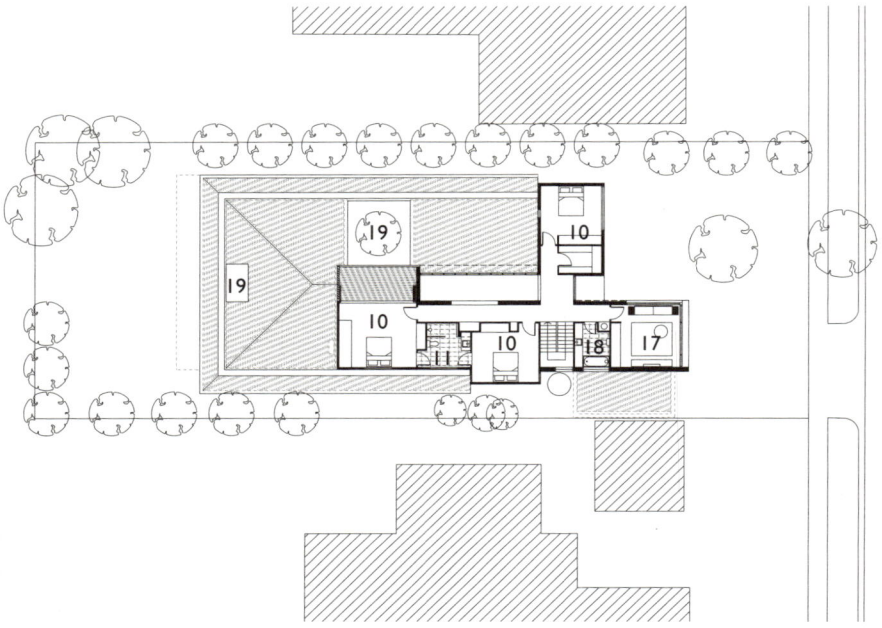

FIRST FLOOR

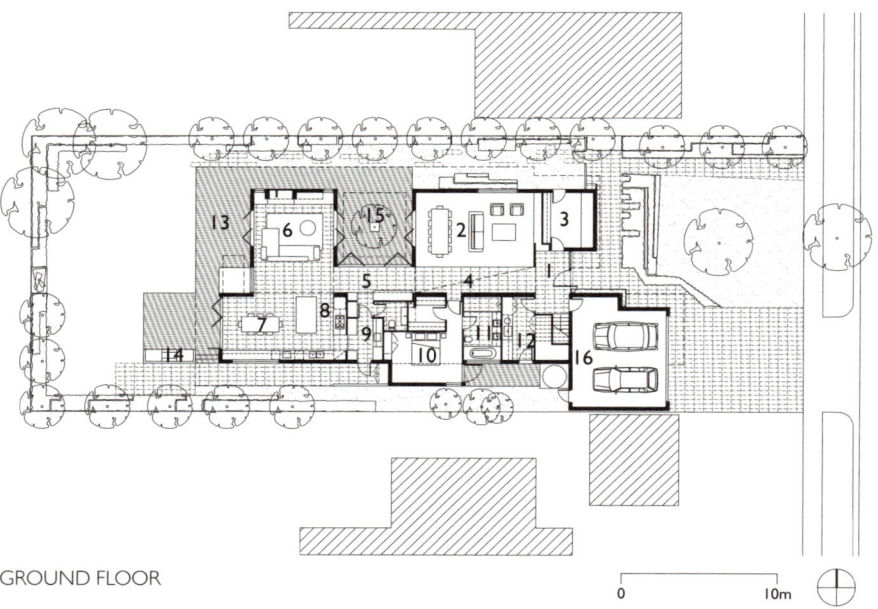

GROUND FLOOR

1 Entry
2 Living area
3 Study
4 Gallery
5 Reading alcove
6 Family area
7 Dining
8 Kitchen
9 Service kitchen
10 Bedroom
11 Ensuite
12 Laundry
13 Deck
14 Barbecue
15 Courtyard
16 Garage
17 Rumpus room
18 Bathroom
19 Void

MoToR

ANDREW SIMPSON ARCHITECTS

Located at Port Fairy, Victoria, three-and-a-half-hours' drive from Melbourne, this house wasn't the typical weekender with panoramic views of the beach. Designed by architect Andrew Simpson, who worked closely with architect Owen West, the idea for the house came from empty nesters taking to the road as they approach their retirement years. "The Australian dream for many retirees is to jump in a caravan and travel the entire continent", says Simpson. ■ Simpson's clients wanted a weekender rather than spend time on the road. But as the Port Fairy site is simply a suburban site in the township, it seemed appropriate to create that sense of freedom in the architecture. ■ The Port Fairy house, elevated on steel poles, is partially clad in black polycarbonate. "We obviously love black, but in this instance it was used to diffuse the light as well as screen a neighbouring home", says Simpson. To further diffuse the light, the architects created a secondary 'skin' of clear polycarbonate. A gap between these two layers purges hot air during the warmer months. The external black polycarbonate wall, which appears to wrap around the roof, also slightly twists. "We saw this form like the canvas awning you often see attached to caravans", says Simpson. ■ This 'awning', like the annex to a caravan, contains the open-plan kitchen and living areas that lead to a large protected terrace. And on a slightly lower level, delineated by a grey fibro-cement clad box, are the bedrooms, including the main bedroom. As the brief required flexible bedrooms, depending on the number of people staying, Simpson and West designed one of the bedrooms to be used in its entirety or divided into two by means of an operable wall that disappears into joinery. ■ While the interior of the Port Fairy house is predominantly white, the architects included black powder-coated window frames in all rooms. These irregular shaped frames/windows also activate the minimal interior. A black flue attached to the fireplace in the living area also creates a graphic quality to the design. ■ "Black isn't a logical colour choice, particularly if an area experiences high temperatures, but there are ways of modifying the colour", says Simpson. "Many architects, given a choice, prefer black rather than steering towards colour", he adds. ■ PHOTOGRAPHY: CHRISTINE FRANCIS

1 Entry
2 Living
3 Dining
4 Kitchen
5 Study
6 Bedroom
7 Bathroom
8 Deck

BLACK

STEVENS LAWSON ARCHITECTS

SEA

Located at one of New Zealand's most popular beaches – Hot Water Beach, whose name derives from hot springs which filter up through the sand – this house was previously part of a caravan park. The owner of the caravan and tent site decided to subdivide the beachfront property and build a home for himself, his wife and their grown-up children, on one of the largest parcels, approximately 2,000 square metres in area, designed by Stevens Lawson Architects. "This is their permanent home, but they wanted an informal design, like a beach house", says architect Nicholas Stevens, who worked closely with fellow director, Gary Lawson. ■ The single-storey house is fully clad in cedar, stained black. The only elements not stained black are the alcoves of the verandahs, which are stained dark brown. "It's similar to biting into an apple and seeing a different colour. But the brown also provides a warmer colour as you enter the different wings", says Stevens. ■ The Hot Water house is divided into two wings. One wing includes the kitchen, dining and living areas, with a dark stained timber battened screen separating the dining area from the living area. This wing also includes a study, as well as a rumpus room, which has both a television and pool table. The second wing is for the children: as they are grown-up, the owner wanted a separate wing for them, which comprises three bedrooms and bathrooms. Linking the two pavilions is a glazed breezeway with coloured glass panels either side. "The colour creates magical effects at various times of the day with the sunlight coming through", says Stevens. The glazed link also provides protection for an internal courtyard. ■ Stevens Lawson Architects regularly design black homes. "Black houses are extremely popular in rural New Zealand, as well as along the coast. There's a tradition of using creosote (a bitumen product)", says Stevens. ■ This particular house called out for a black treatment, being on the edge of a pristine beach. "It's an extremely sensitive site, so we wanted the house to blend in with the trees and appear recessive to the beach", adds Stevens. "The house is low slung so it doesn't affect the environment", he adds. ■ PHOTOGRAPHY: MARK SMITH

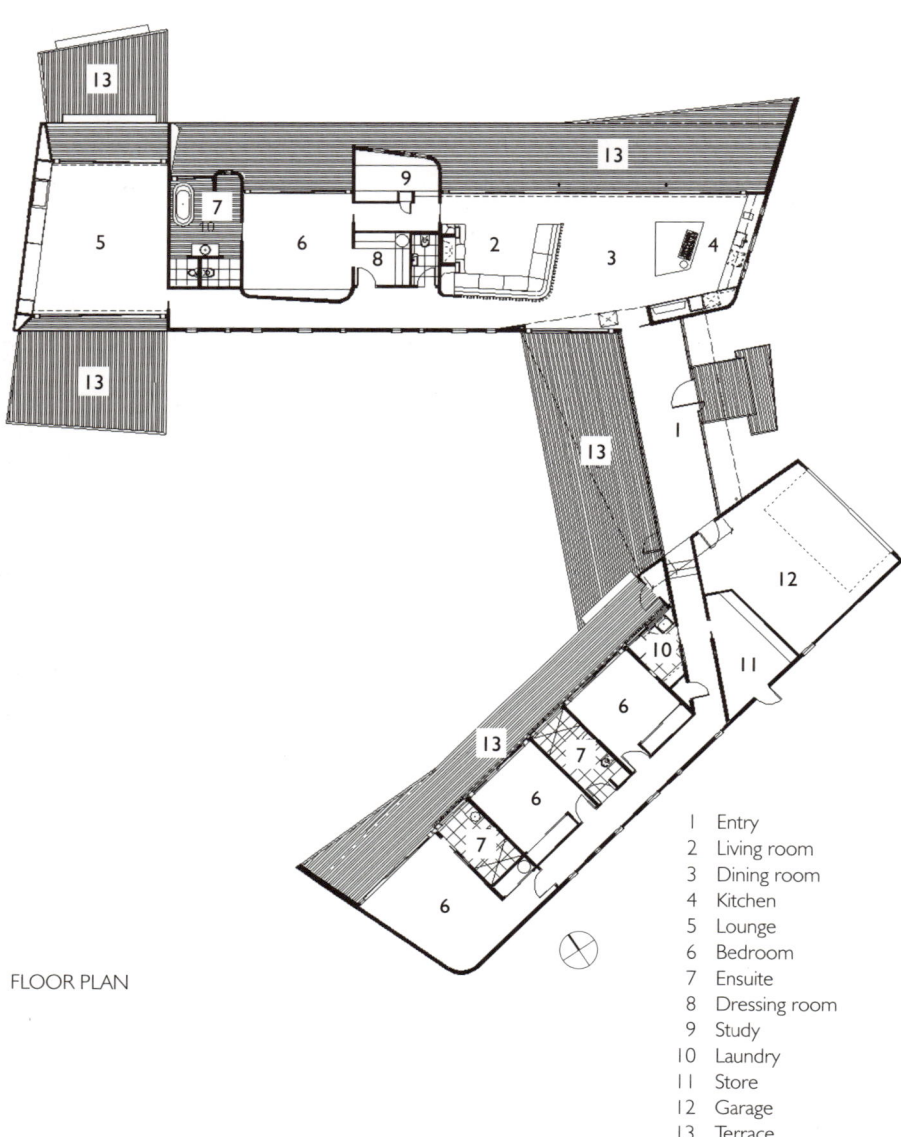

FLOOR PLAN

1 Entry
2 Living room
3 Dining room
4 Kitchen
5 Lounge
6 Bedroom
7 Ensuite
8 Dressing room
9 Study
10 Laundry
11 Store
12 Garage
13 Terrace

POiNT

CASE ORNSBY AND TOBIN SMITH

OF VIEW

This simple and understated house is on the Banks Peninsula, an hour's drive from Christchurch, New Zealand. Created by Case Ornsby together with designer Tobin Smith, the brief for this weekender was to create 'a sense of camping'. "Our clients wanted a house that was significantly different from their permanent home in Christchurch", says Ornsby. "But Tobin and I were also conscious of the modest homes in the area", he adds. ■ Located on a relatively steep site on the water's edge, the single-storey house (approximately 120 square metres in area) is predominantly clad in cedar, stained black. Only the garage and detached bunkroom are made from concrete blocks. "For this section, we had to excavate. It made sense to use concrete rather than timber", says Ornsby. The designers considered several options before deciding on stained black cedar; they were drawn to black for its recessive qualities. "We also wanted to be able to control the colour. If we allowed unstained timber to respond to the weather, it could end up any shade", says Ornsby. ■ The house centres on an internal courtyard, with an open-plan kitchen and living areas on one side and two bedrooms of identical scale providing two protective arms. "It can get extremely windy here. You need to be able to have a place to sit outside all year around", says Ornsby. To ensure transparency and a view over the water, large sliding glass doors frame the living pavilion. ■ One of the more unusual aspects of the design is the location of all three bedrooms (including the concrete bunkroom). These rooms can be accessed only by walking outside the living areas. "Our clients wanted that sense of camping, of enjoying the weather and the surrounds first hand", says Ornsby. ■ In contrast to the almost all-black exterior, the interior is predominantly white. Only the kitchen joinery and central-island bench, in black veneer timber, are a contrast to the colour palette. "We've tried to keep the interior as light as possible to reflect the light", says Ornsby. "It's also about having a contrast to the dark exterior", he adds. ■ PHOTOGRAPHY: STEPHEN GOODENOUGH

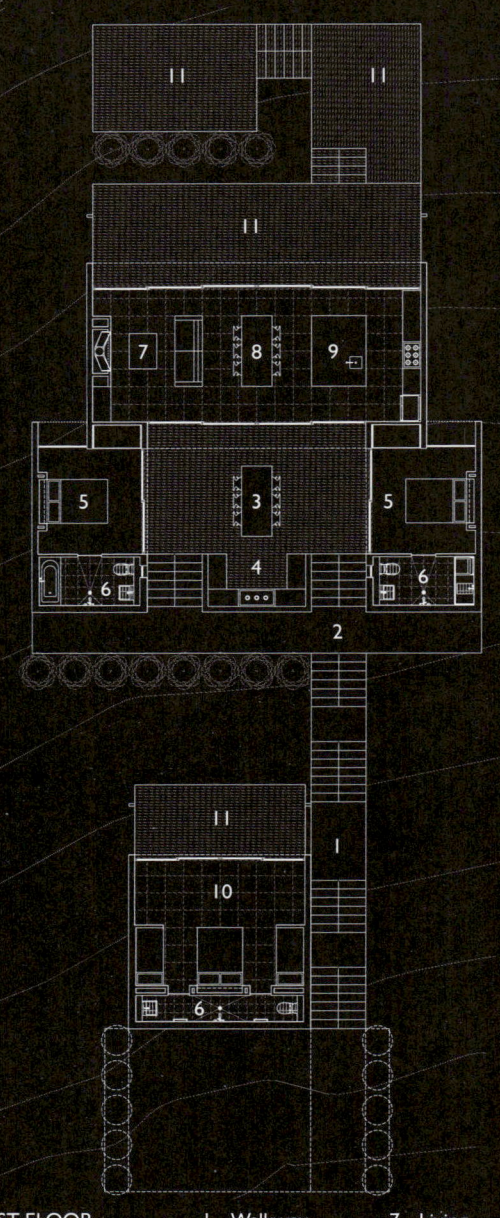

FIRST FLOOR

1 Walkway
2 Entry
3 Terrace
4 Outdoor fire
5 Bedroom
6 Ensuite
7 Living
8 Dining
9 Kitchen
10 Bunkroom
11 Deck

Stained

1+2 ARCHITECTURE

Designed by 1+2 Architecture, this black house is located at Mount Nelson, a suburb on the fringe of Hobart. "Mount Nelson is one of the higher points in Hobart, 400 metres above sea level. It's almost a different climate, with snow periodically falling through winter", says architect Fred Ward, a director of the practice. ■ While the climate was an important trigger to their design, so was the house next door, a white house designed in the 1970s by architect Michael Viney. "Viney was a great exponent of white houses. We thought designing a black house would complement his design", says Ward. The design of this house was also influenced by the shape of the site, which is relatively compact and wine glass-shaped. ■ The site, which has a fall across the site of approximately 1.5 metres, also features a rocky outcrop terrain. As excavating would be difficult, the architects designed a single-storey house with a generous void over the living area. "There are height restrictions in the area so we couldn't include a second level", says Ward. ■ The Mount Nelson house was constructed using concrete blockwork to anchor the building to the rocky terrain. Stained timber cladding features on the remainder of the external walls. "The macrocarpa (timber) is extremely durable and has a wonderful knotty grain", says Ward. "Our clients wanted a fairly low-maintenance house as they both work, so they were keen for us to use durable and robust materials", he adds. ■ The irregular-shaped house includes three bedrooms, as well as two living areas – one formal, the other more casual. The kitchen forms part of the open-plan living area. In contrast to the black exterior, the kitchen is of a relatively pale colour. The kitchen joinery, for example, is made from hoop pine. There are, however, black accents through the kitchen and living areas such as black stained plywood below the central island bench and in the form of a black glass splashback. Black also appears in the laminate used to line some of the bookshelves. ■ The choice of black wasn't simply to 'speak' to the neighbouring home. The architects were also mindful of the snow-covered ground through the winter months. "We wanted to create a heavier protective shell. It also helps articulate the areas where we've used white, such as the point of entry", adds Ward. ■ PHOTOGRAPHY: JONATHAN WHERRETT

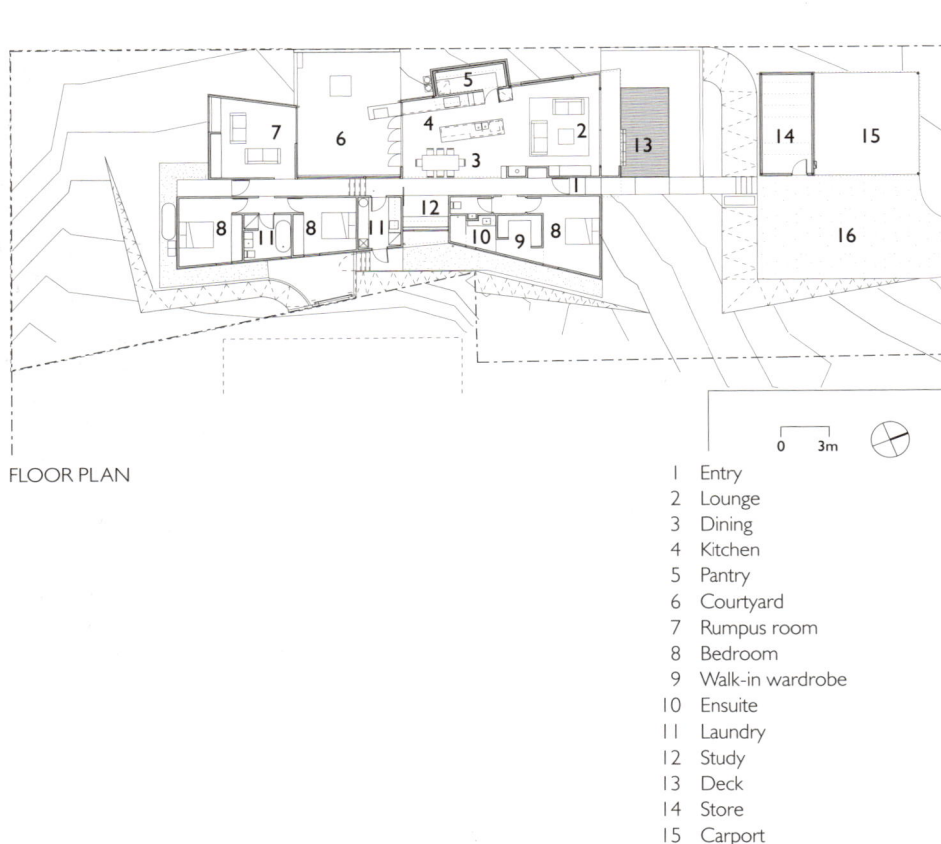

FLOOR PLAN

1 Entry
2 Lounge
3 Dining
4 Kitchen
5 Pantry
6 Courtyard
7 Rumpus room
8 Bedroom
9 Walk-in wardrobe
10 Ensuite
11 Laundry
12 Study
13 Deck
14 Store
15 Carport
16 Driveway

LIGHT

MATTER

Designed by Matter, this house at Whiritoa, on the Coromandel Peninsula, New Zealand, is deliberately lightweight. Located on a flood plain, the architects also had to deal with a public drain that ran across the 300-square-metre property. "It's the lowest point in the area. We had to ensure the house was two-and-a-half metres above ground level", says architect Adrian McNaught, one of three directors of Matter. McNaught worked closely with John Holley, the principal designer of this house. ■ Holley was drawn to the simple black homes of the 1950s and '60s designed by New Zealand architect Vernon Brown. "Brown designed several black houses on the North Island using black creosote (a bitumen product used for the protection of timber). He would often contrast the creosote with white window frames", says McNaught. ■ Instead of creosote, Matter used plywood, stained black, for this house. The central element contains an open-plan kitchen and living areas that lead to a deck. At ground level, there's also a bathroom and two bedroom alcoves, just large enough for two double beds. "We saw the ground level like a wharf", says McNaught, pointing out the broad timber deck adjacent to the living areas. ■ On either side of the house are two towering elements. One, wrapped in translucent polycarbonate, contains the stairwell to a roof terrace. On the other side of the house is the fireplace, clad in zincalume. "These elements are certainly magnified by the stained black timber", says McNaught. ■ As the house, like many other properties in this area, is wedged between sand dunes, Matter was keen to create a large open terrace on the roof. This allows for unimpeded views of the Pacific Ocean. "It's a very modest house, probably no more than 80 square metres. John (Holley) was keen from the outset to follow Brown's path rather than simply produce McMansions along the coast", adds McNaught. ■ PHOTOGRAPHY: ADRIAN McNAUGHT

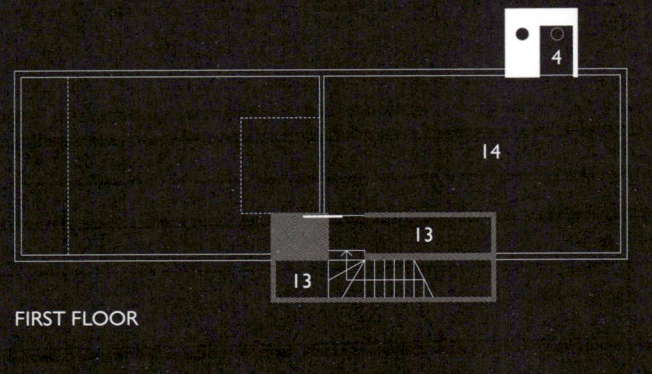

1 Entry stair
2 Living
3 Kitchen
4 Fire
5 Bedroom
6 Shower
7 Water closet
8 Rear deck
9 Drawbridge
10 Deck
11 Laundry
12 Stair
13 Store
14 Roof deck

FIRST FLOOR

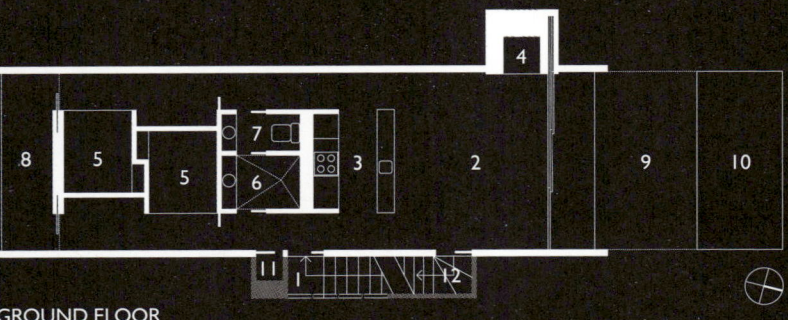

GROUND FLOOR

BLACK

JASON BAILEY ARCHITECTURE + DESIGN MANAGEMENT

FOREST

Surrounded by bush, this black timber house is both home and office for architect Jason Bailey. Previously Bailey was living in an apartment in Auckland and using this beach house only at weekends. However, as this house, located at Piha, is only a forty-five minute drive from Auckland, Bailey decided to sell the apartment and live and work from this picturesque coastal village. ■ While Piha is close to Auckland, there are strict building controls as a result of the area's sensitive environment. "I don't think I would have obtained permission to build an entirely new house", says Bailey. So rather than starting from scratch, Bailey used some of the structure from a 1980s house previously built on this site. "The '80s house was quite basic. But I was able to retain some of the structural foundations, including some of the flooring". ■ Bailey replaced the '80s house with a simple two-storey building, clad in western red cedar and stained black. The roof, like the house, is recessive, made from steel in a charcoal-black hue. The window- and doorframes are also black, made from powder-coated aluminium. "I wanted this house to disappear into the environment as much as possible. After all, it's more about the view", says Bailey, pointing out the landmark rock – the Lion Rock, overlooking the Tasman Sea. ■ The home's black exterior also provides a contrast to the home's essentially all-white interior. At ground level, with its own point of entry, is Bailey's studio, together with guest accommodation. On the first floor, also with its own entrance, are the kitchen and the living areas, together with main bedroom and bathroom. "It's a fairly modest project, not much more than 100 square metres combined", says Bailey, who estimates his home to be approximately the same size as the apartment he left behind in Auckland. "But this place feels considerably more spacious", adds Bailey, referring to the terraces and surrounding bush. ■ Bailey not only appreciates the views from both home and at work, he also enjoys seeing the house recede into the bush. "Black creates a continuous object. You're not distracted by superfluous detail", adds Bailey. ■ PHOTOGRAPHY: KALLAN MACLEOD

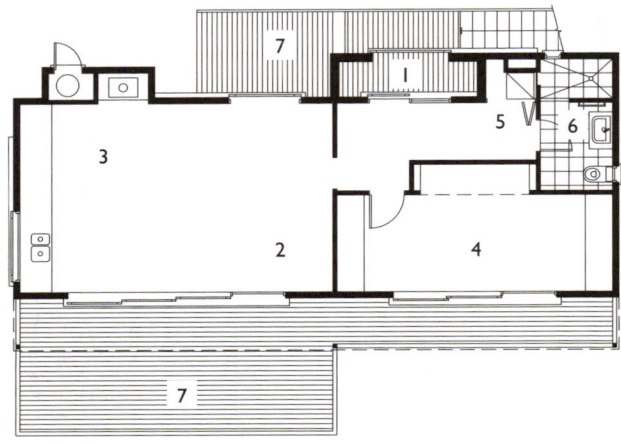

UPPER FLOOR

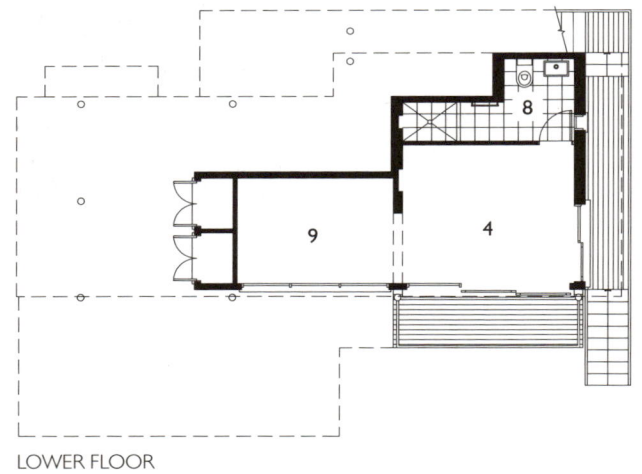

LOWER FLOOR

1 Entry
2 Living
3 Kitchen
4 Bedroom
5 Laundry
6 Bathroom
7 Deck
8 Ensuite
9 Study

SHINGLE

NORD ARCHITECTURE

Designed by Nord Architecture, this black house, known as the 'Shingle House', is located in Dungeness, on the south-east coast of England. A place without walls or fences, it is Britain's only 'desert'. And among the tiny fishermen's huts are these pitched black forms. ■ The starting point in designing this new house was to ensure it stood up to the adverse climatic conditions, with extreme temperatures, exposure to wind and salt spray, as well as frequent drought. The superstructure of the house consists of a closed timber kit built around a 150-square-metre concrete slab and a concrete spine with chimney, stair, hearth, kitchen and bath. The house is clad in timber shingles and vertical board with a black 'tar' protective coat. "The red cedar timber shingles and red cedar vertical timber cladding are pre-coated with falun black paint prior to application, then a second and third coat are applied post-fixing", says architect Mark Bell, project architect at Nord Architecture. ■ "The blackness of Dungeness can be seen in a variety of sheds, huts, garages, storage containers and boats", says Bell. Black also has a historical relationship with people on this part of the coast, who use tar paper and pine tar as a protective coating on the shacks and cottages. ■ While the Shingle House 'speaks' to its neighbours in terms of form and colour, black has also been used inside the home with selected fixtures and furnishings and as a contrast to the all-white interior, in the form of textured timber boards. Bespoke black timber hanging pegs are set out on the timber-lined walls and there are black electrical sockets and switches. Bespoke black-stained timber door handles feature in the house, as well as black light fittings. ■ Like the inclement weather, Shingle House responds to the changing seasons, opening up to expose the views and welcome human habitation, but able to close itself off from its surroundings. "A series of shutters can seal the house from the drama of the weather, offering a protective skin and providing the most basic form of shelter", adds Bell. ■ PHOTOGRAPHY: CHARLES HOSEA AND LIVING ARCHITECTURE

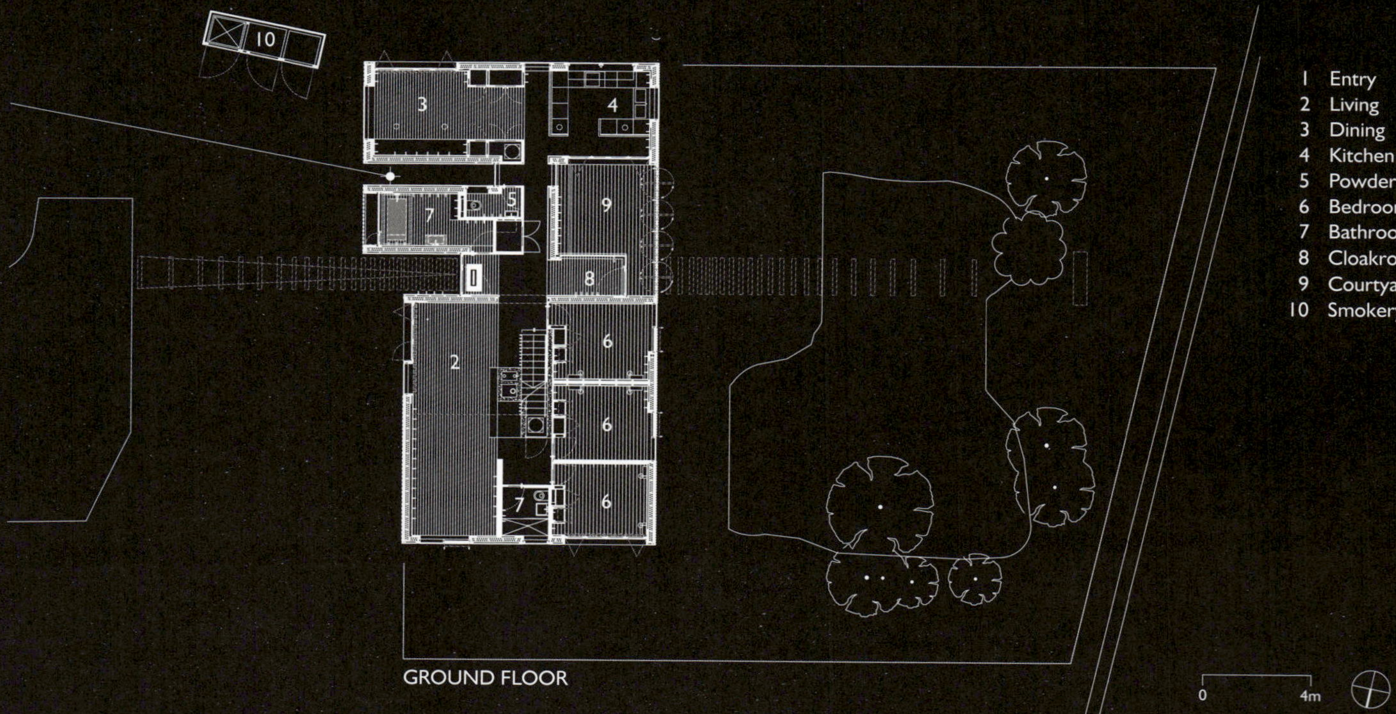

1. Entry
2. Living
3. Dining
4. Kitchen
5. Powder room
6. Bedroom
7. Bathroom
8. Cloakroom
9. Courtyard
10. Smokery

GROUND FLOOR

NIGHT

KENNEDY NOLAN ARCHITECTS

This modest timber home, built between the wars, was originally only 100 square metres in area. "Our clients wanted us to design a family home. Their initial thoughts were to remove the timber house", says architect Patrick Kennedy, who worked closely with fellow director of the firm, architect Rachel Nolan. ■ Kennedy Nolan managed to convince the owners that the house was structurally sound and could be integrated into a larger family home. "Some of the detail in the original home is quite impressive", says Kennedy, referring to the hardwood flooring and wall panels, together with ornate art deco style plaster ceilings. ■ The original home, which features a formal lounge, two bedrooms and a bathroom, was restored. However, past the double doors of the lounge, the level of the floor drops just over one metre. "The main problem with the house was the slope of the site. There was essentially no connection with the garden from the rear", says Kennedy. ■ In contrast to the smaller rooms in the original home, the extension, clad in timber painted high-gloss black, is spacious. The new wing includes a kitchen and large family room that leads to the garden. The 3.6-metre-long kitchen bench was conceived as a refined object in the open-plan space. Mounted on a black steel frame, the marble bench creates a sculptural effect. ■ The family room is rich in texture rather than colour. Random-sized timber columns, stained black, frame floor-to-ceiling glass windows to the garden. "We saw these columns as being like a forest. They frame various aspects of the garden", says Nolan, who also lowered the ceiling height over the family room to elongate the space and draw views beyond the perimeter of the house. ■ The extension, clad in treated pine and painted in high-gloss black paint, is reminiscent of a grand piano. With its curvaceous form, it's a refreshing alternative to the rectilinear glass box used in many alterations and extensions. "We've used this piano shape on several of our designs. In this case, we were able to frame the oak tree as well as provide an organic shape that responded to this site", says Kennedy. "We also wanted the two structures (old and new) to appear as a single object, rather than two competing forms", adds Kennedy. ■ PHOTOGRAPHY: DEREK SWALWELL

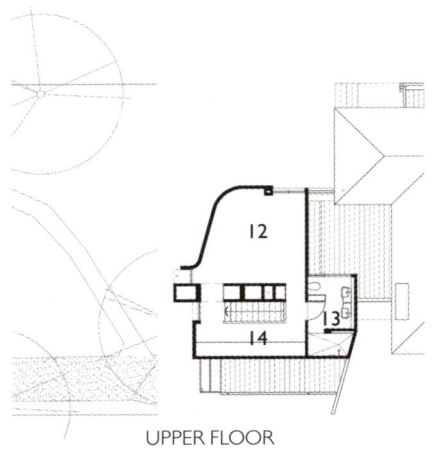

UPPER FLOOR

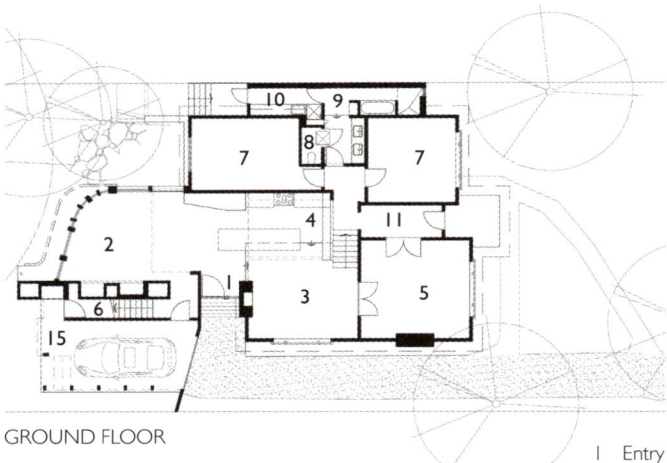

GROUND FLOOR

0 5m

1 Entry
2 Living room
3 Dining room
4 Kitchen
5 Sitting room
6 Store
7 Bedroom
8 Powder room
9 Bathroom
10 Laundry
11 Hall
12 Master bedroom
13 Master ensuite
14 Dressing room
15 Carport

LOVE

XSITE ARCHITECTS

Located at Russell, on New Zealand's Bay of Islands, this one-bedroom house is fully clad in band sawn cedar, stained black. As the house is situated on a prominent point overlooking Te Whapau Bay, the architect, XSite Architects, wanted to make the house appear as recessive as possible. "We wanted the house to disappear into the landscape", says architect Malcolm Taylor, director of the practice. ■ Like many New Zealand architects, the black house was partially inspired by the late architect Vernon Brown. Like Brown's designs, where many of his homes were framed in white timber, XSite's house features white window frames and detailing such as columns and under eaves. XSite also painted the exposed timber ceilings white. While the roof isn't black, it's a dark green, like the pine trees framing the house. ■ The split-level home – intended as a kind of self-contained 'hotel room' and getaway for couples to escape crying kids and dirty nappies, hence its nickname 'Love Shack' – follows the contours of the land. The main living area, which leads to a deck via stackable glass doors, features a double-height void. The main mezzanine-style bedroom overlooks the living areas. "The house was designed as a weekender. It's quite a simple layout", says Taylor. ■ While the exterior of the house is black, the interior is animated by vivid coloured wallpapers, evocative of the 1950s and '60s. Framing the wallpapered walls are expressed black beams and a bracing wall in the living area, made from band sawn plywood, stained black. ■ Dark stains were also used for the kitchen joinery, with Wenge veneers on the kitchen joinery complementing the perforated Formica used on some of the cupboards. "It's a fairly graphic house", says Taylor, referring to the staircase. ■ The retreat is clad in low-maintenance horizontal bevel-back weatherboards. "The choice of the materials is predominantly to exaggerate the change in the plane on the north face, as the building diminishes in width. Black also has the effect of reducing the scale of the structure", adds Taylor. ■ PHOTOGRAPHY: MALCOLM TAYLOR

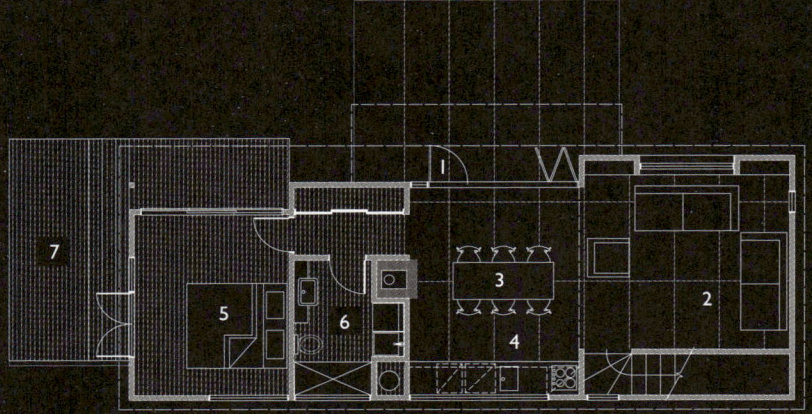

FLOOR PLAN

1 Entry
2 Living
3 Dining
4 Kitchen
5 Bedroom
6 Bathroom/laundry
7 Deck

INK G

JOHN WARDLE ARCHITECTS

This striking contemporary home conceals the few remnants of a house designed in the 1950s by architect Horace Tribe. Completely remodeled in stages, the only thing that remains of the original design are a few walls and two established Scottish Elm trees, almost one hundred years old. "There's very little remaining", says architect John Wardle, who lives in this house with his family. ■ While some of the walls of the two-storey house are rendered masonry and grey zinc, the house is predominantly clad in stained black timber, in a board-and-batten arrangement. Rather than simply fasten the battens from the outside, Wardle devised an ingenious solution of attaching all the screws from a neoprene gasket layer concealed behind. "I didn't want any visible fixtures. I wanted the focus to be the textures of the bark on the elm trees", says Wardle. ■ As well as black-stained timber used for the exterior, Wardle's house includes black steel for the structural frame, together with black window frames. The garage door, which blends into the façade, is made of plywood, painted black. "The two elms initiated the design. I consulted a tree surgeon from the outset to see how close we could go to the trees without disturbing them", says Wardle. ■ As a consequence, the front portion of Wardle's house 'slips' between the trees. And to frame each tree, there are large picture windows, some elongated in shape to take in the massive trunks. The materials used inside the home also build on the texture of the trees. The study, for example, is framed by a wicker balustrade. However, in contrast to the moody exterior, the interior is predominantly white and lighter in palette, with pure white walls and pale timber floors. ■ Wardle has designed several black houses. Each time, there's a different reason for using black. "Black tends to abstract a design. Rather than simply becoming a house, black makes it feel more akin to an object sitting in the landscape, be it a city, rural or coastal environment", adds Wardle. ■ PHOTOGRAPHY: TREVOR MEIN

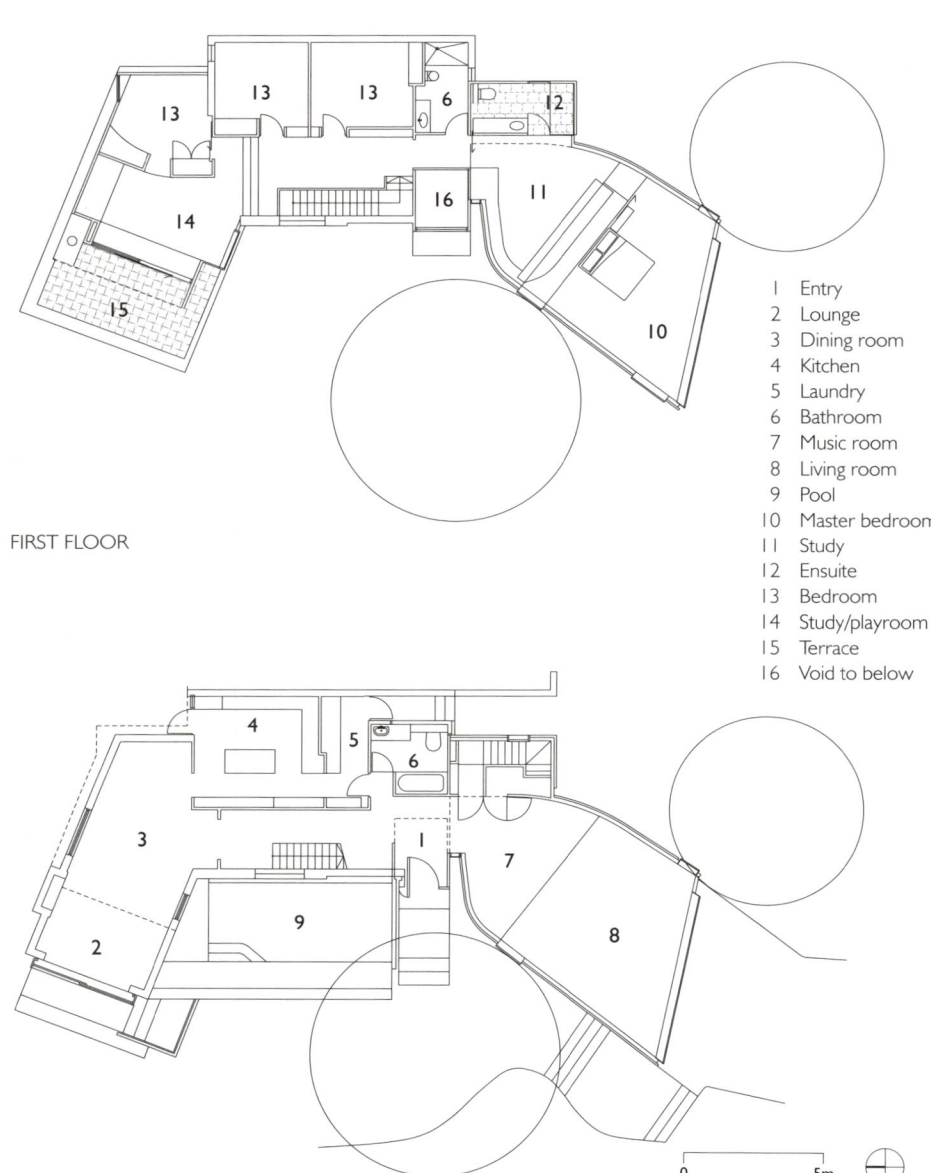

FIRST FLOOR

1 Entry
2 Lounge
3 Dining room
4 Kitchen
5 Laundry
6 Bathroom
7 Music room
8 Living room
9 Pool
10 Master bedroom
11 Study
12 Ensuite
13 Bedroom
14 Study/playroom
15 Terrace
16 Void to below

GROUND FLOOR

ReNdeR

DAVID EDELMAN ARCHITECTS

Originally this house was single-storey and cream brick. Built in the 1960s, it wasn't suitable for a family with four children. However, rather than demolish the entire house, architect David Edelman retained the front two rooms, originally the dining and living areas. He also retained the angular front windows, but reframed these in aluminium. ■ Edelman added open-plan living areas to the ground floor, as well as an alfresco indoor–outdoor room. He also included a bathroom adjacent to a rumpus room/guest bedroom to allow for live-in help while the children are still young. On the first floor are five bedrooms and bathrooms. ■ As the original home extended almost from boundary to boundary, Edelman wasn't able to provide a garage. The solution was to create a canopy over the front forecourt, large enough to accommodate two cars. Three-and-a-half metres wide, this canopy appears to 'float' above the entrance to the home. "The canopy gives the house quite a sculptural feel", says Edelman, who also designed a high rendered black front fence, with planter boxes. Planted with Manchurian pear trees, the colours of the leaves, from gold to plum, appear more intense against the black walls. "The venetian blinds (above the canopy) are also black to create a uniform façade", adds Edelman. ■ In contrast to the black exterior, the interior is relatively light in palette. Pale timber veneer for walls and limed oak floors complement materials such as silver travertine for the kitchen benchtops. "Lighter coloured floors are more practical when you've got young children. You don't tend to notice scratches", says Edelman. ■ One of the most dramatic areas of the house is the outdoor terrace, complete with barbecue, adjacent to the family room. As well as having a black painted feature wall, there are supersized graphics of leaves extending across one entire wall. "Black works particularly well with colour. But black also sharpens a form", adds Edelman. ■ PHOTOGRAPHY: DEAN SCHMIDEG

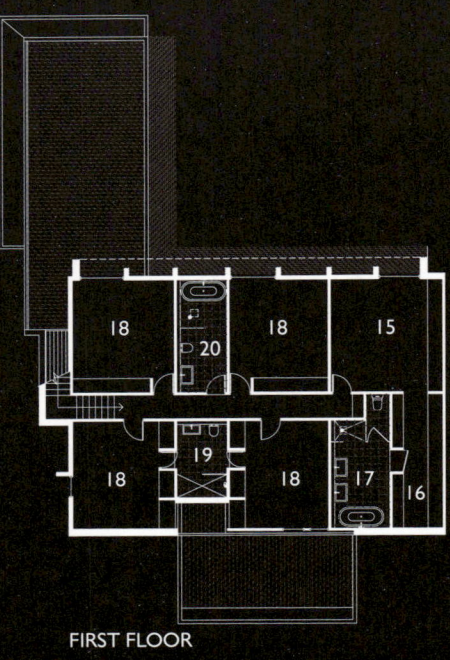
FIRST FLOOR

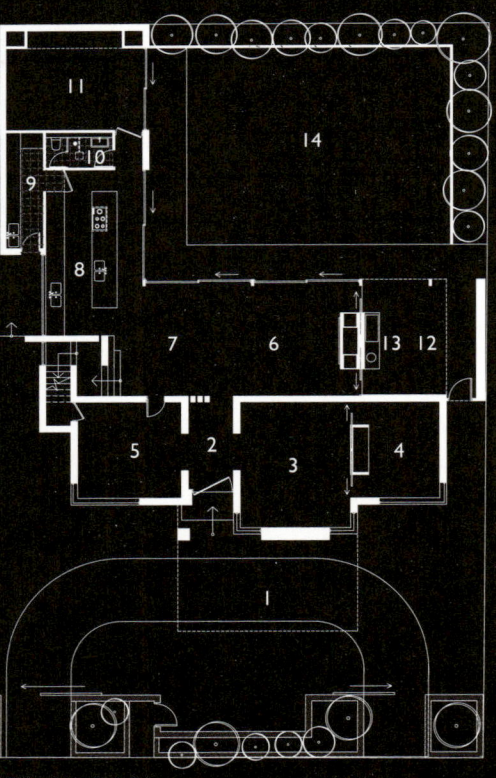
GROUND FLOOR

1 Portico
2 Entry
3 Living room
4 Study
5 Dining room
6 Family area
7 Breakfast area
8 Kitchen
9 Laundry
10 Powder room
11 Guest room/play room
12 Alfresco dining
13 Barbecue
14 Lawn
15 Master bedroom
16 Walk-in wardrobe
17 Master ensuite
18 Bedroom
19 Ensuite
20 Bathroom

DARK

STRACHAN GROUP ARCHITECTS

Designed for a couple approaching retirement, this house on New Zealand's Waiheke Island is located on a sensitive ridge line. Surrounded by native bush and overlooking Owhanake Bay, the brief was for a low-slung building that was both recessive in the landscape and single storey. "Our clients didn't want to climb stairs in order to appreciate the surrounds", says architect David Strachan, director of Strachan Group Architects. ■ To ensure the house was recessive in the landscape, Strachan clad the exterior of the house in western red cedar and stained it black. The architects used three different profiles of timber to give the house a more crafted feel. "The pattern is slightly random to add to that crafted look", says Strachan. ■ To create a single-storey building and accommodate all the rooms required, the architect designed a long narrow house, approximately 6 metres wide – essentially only one room wide. Conceived as three pavilions, the house features skillion roofs to maximise natural light. ■ At one end of the Waiheke Island house are two guest bedrooms and a bathroom. At the other end is the main bedroom and an ensuite, together with a studio/office. At the core of the house are an open-plan kitchen and living areas. The architect 'bridged' the three pavilions with interstitial spaces, one containing a plunge pool, the other being an ensuite to the main bedroom. ■ While the exterior of the house is relatively dark, the interior is considerably lighter. Apart from the dark-stained timber portals spanning the living areas, the interior features hoop pine, a pale timber. Dark stained timber ceilings also act as a protective canopy. "We stained the walls along the passage black to further link the interior to the outdoors", says Strachan. ■ "There's a long tradition of black houses in New Zealand. It comes from our landscape, recalling Ponga ferns with their black trunks and stems", adds Strachan. ■ PHOTOGRAPHY: PATRICK REYNOLDS

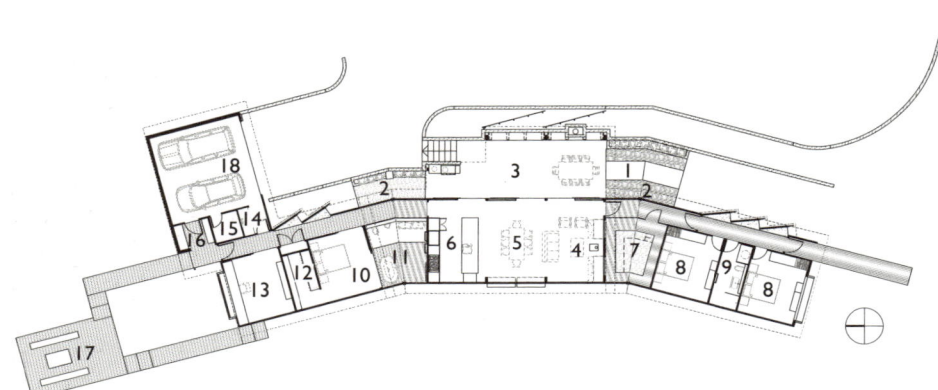

FLOOR PLAN

1 Entry bridge
2 Pond
3 Outdoor room
4 Lounge
5 Dining
6 Kitchen
7 Indoor plunge pool
8 Guest bedroom
9 Guest bathroom
10 Master bedroom
11 Ensuite
12 Walk-in wardrobe
13 Study
14 Laundry
15 Store
16 Rear porch
17 Deck
18 Garage

BLACK

ZOELLER DESIGN

Designed by Joshua Zoeller, this black house sits on the edge of a national park. Three-and-a-half hours' drive from Sydney, on the New South Wales coast, it's a popular tourist destination. "The owners live in Sydney and wanted a weekender that was diametrically opposite to their permanent home", says Zoeller. ■ Unlike their permanent home, which includes internal stairs and passages, this design centres on the outdoors, with an external covered staircase providing the main circulation spine. The house is designed over five levels due to the 20-degree slope. "I wanted to use materials that would lend themselves to the difficult slope, but I was also mindful of the fibre cement holiday homes in the area", says Zoeller. ■ The house features a steel frame for ease of construction and is clad in horizontal bands of concrete fibre cement sheets. With the programme requiring quite a large house, Zoeller wanted to make the house appear as recessive as possible and not dominate the surrounding bush. "There's a lot of cladding, with considerable surface area. The black cement sheets are also economical", says Zoeller. The 30cm-wide bands of cement sheeting assist in anchoring the home to this steep site. ■ At ground level are the garage and laundry. A staircase leads to the outdoor foyer/lobby with a main bedroom and ensuite. Another step leads to the main courtyard, used as an outdoor living area. Zoeller also included the kitchen and main living areas at this level, all enclosed. A further level includes two additional bedrooms and on the top level is a studio, which can function as a guest bedroom. The owner specifically requested a studio for his calligraphy painting. And with a keen interest in Japan, Zoeller included a white pebbled Japanese-style garden outside the studio. ■ This area contains some of the tallest eucalypts in Australia. The majestic pale white tree trunks and the vertical steel structure appear more intense, set against the home's black cladding. "The trees become even more luminescent in the early morning and late in the day", says Zoeller. ■ PHOTOGRAPHY: SIMON WHITBREAD AND ANDREW SHEPHERD

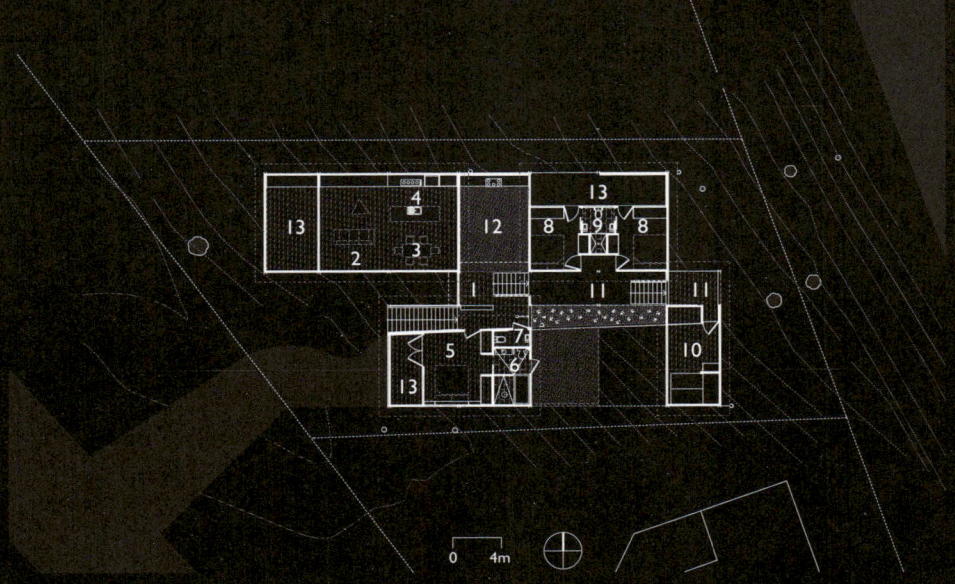

FLOOR PLAN

1 Entry deck
2 Lounge
3 Dining room
4 Kitchen
5 Master bedroom
6 Master ensuite
7 Powder room
8 Bedroom
9 Ensuite
10 Workshop/office
11 Promenade
12 Winter courtyard
13 Deck

LIGHT &

1+2 ARCHITECTURE

Many homes surrounding Hobart's Derwent River face the dilemma of having great views, but not being able to share those views with full sunlight. It was this concern that steered the design of this home by 1+2 Architecture. "We didn't want too many windows facing the river as this would release too much heat", says architect Fred Ward, one of three directors of the practice. ■ This single-storey house, located at Lindisfarne on the eastern shore, is low-slung to frame views, as well as create a warm interior. "We were also conscious of the budget and not exceeding it", says Ward, who created a simple black pavilion. Like other homes they've designed, the Lindisfarne house is made from concrete blocks, stained black timber cladding, fibre cement sheeting and stained dark charcoal. Large timber decks on either side of the house provide both the view of the river as well as the benefit of enjoying full sunlight. ■ The three-bedroom house, with skillion-shaped roof, is split-level. The main living area, for example, is a few steps below the kitchen and dining area. "We've essentially followed the contours of the land, reducing the need to excavate", says Ward, referring to the rocky outcrops on the site. ■ While black features extensively on the home's exterior, the interior is predominantly white. There are, however, black structural beams, which are expressed in the living areas. Black mosaic glass tiles also surround the fireplace in the living room, as well as on the plinth, which extends across the room. Black carpets also appear in many of the rooms. ■ "We often use black, whether it's the exterior or interior", says Ward, who sees black as ideal for a bushland setting. "Black becomes like the shadows of the bush. Unlike green, say, which appears in foliage, but stands out", he adds. And in time, the black timber will soften in tone, becoming more charcoal in colour, like the surrounding tree trunks. ■ PHOTOGRAPHY: JONATHAN WHERRETT

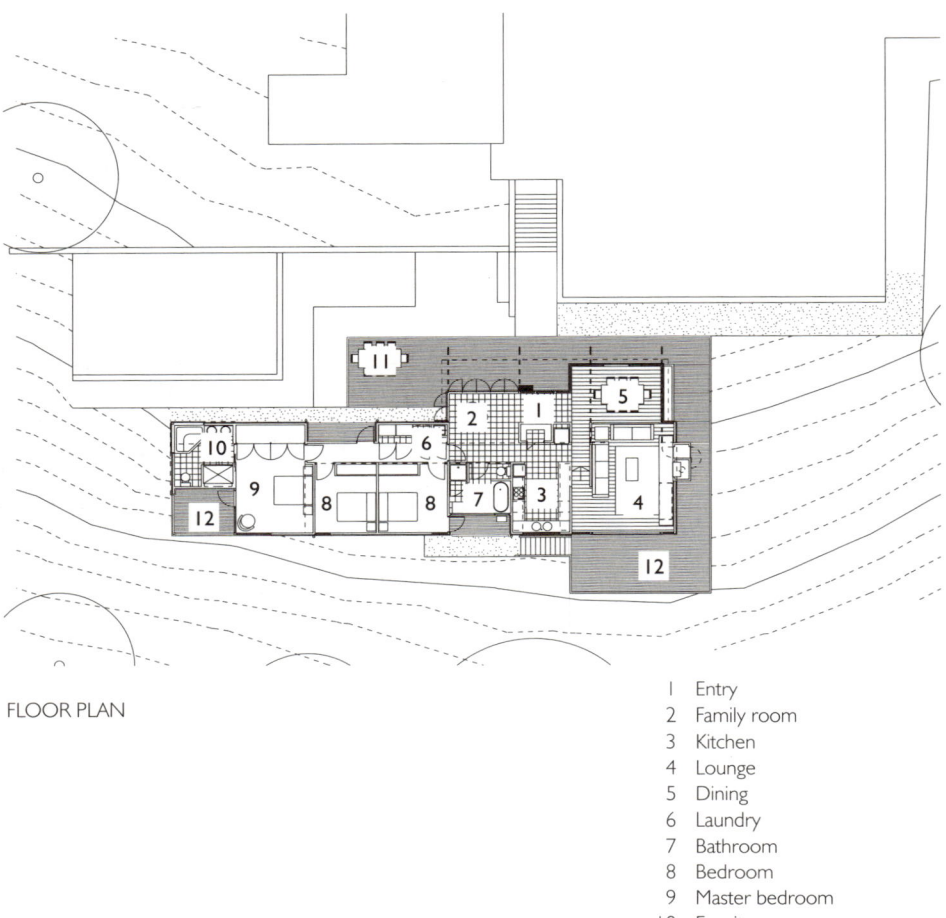

FLOOR PLAN

1 Entry
2 Family room
3 Kitchen
4 Lounge
5 Dining
6 Laundry
7 Bathroom
8 Bedroom
9 Master bedroom
10 Ensuite
11 Outdoor living area
12 Deck

SHADES

INARC ARCHITECTS

This home, in a leafy street, is one of the few single-storey homes in the neighbourhood. While the home was designed for a family, a covenant on the property prevented the architects from adding a first floor. Fortunately, local council guidelines allowed Inarc Architects to excavate below ground level to create basement car parking and room for storage, plant and equipment. "This allowed us to free up the boundaries for landscaping rather than using this area for equipment", says architect Reno Rizzo, director of the practice. ■ The house features a high gabion-walled fence to the street, and just discernable is the striking charcoal black zinc façade. "Many of the older houses in the street have slate roofs. We thought it was appropriate to use zinc, a contemporary material, but of a similar colour to the pitched roofs surrounding this house", says Rizzo. To further articulate the home's façade, as well as defining points of entry, Inarc Architects created a number of 'cut-outs' in the zinc. One 'cut-out' frames a large glass pivot door to the terrace and swimming pool in the front garden. ■ To further animate the black grey façade, the architects included burnt orange painted timber frames for the main openings. "The orange adds relief to the fairly monochromatic palette", says Rizzo. ■ Inside, the spacious house is loosely divided into kitchen and living areas across the front, as well as a large study used by the entire family. "The study receives the most light, but it also provides an important connection to the street", says Rizzo, pointing out the sight lines above the rock wall. ■ The other wings include bedrooms, as well as the main bedroom and ensuite, which extend across almost the entire rear of the property. And like the façade, the interior, apart from some vibrant red shelving, is monochrome, with grey tiled floors and pale grey joinery. Rizzo regularly uses black materials in his designs. For this particular house, the black zinc panels are each a slightly different shade. "They add depth to the façade and provide a sense of subtlety", he adds. ■ PHOTOGRAPHY: PETER CLARKE

5 Dining
6 Kitchen
7 Pantry
8 Laundry
9 Powder room
10 Master bedroom
11 Walk-in wardrobe
12 Master ensuite
13 Bedroom
14 Ensuite
15 Study
16 Terrace
17 Pool

BLACK

dKO ARCHITECTURE

This inner-city house is known as the 'black house' by locals. Featuring ship lap cedar at ground level, the first floor is crisply defined with a typical pitched roof. Made from black steel, the house creates a sharp contrast against blue sky. "The shape of this townhouse was partially the result of the local council's guidelines", says Architect Jesse Linardi, a director of dKO Architecture. "Council wanted the house to be sympathetic to the Victorian cottages lining the street", he adds. ■ The corner site, approximately 270 square metres, was subdivided into two lots to create two townhouses. While this townhouse features an all black-clad first floor, the neighbouring townhouse features a ground floor clad in Cypress stained black, with the first floor made from white steel. "I wanted the two houses to share a common 'language', rather than being identical, like many townhouses", says Linardi. ■ For the 'black house', dKO Architecture also used black aluminium window and door frames. And to protect the house from the afternoon sunlight, the architects designed a series of perforated steel 'hoods' to frame windows. ■ On the ground floor of this townhouse (approximately 115 square metres in area), are three bedrooms and two bathrooms. And to maximise natural light, dKO Architects located the living areas on the first floor. A staircase separates the kitchen and dining area from the living area, which leads to a balcony. There's also a small room adjacent to the kitchen for watching television. "I didn't want the television to dominate the living areas", says Linardi. ■ In contrast to the all-black form of the first floor, the interior is predominantly white. The only black features are the window and doorframes, accentuating the home's pitched form. Black laminate also appears in some of the joinery in the galley-style kitchen. And to lighten the palette, the architects used pale timber on the floors throughout. ■ To add texture to the home's exterior, Linardi selected black ribbed steel. "This creates light and shade, as well as depth", he adds. ■ PHOTOGRAPHY: DEREK SWALWELL

NIGHT ON

BOCHSLER + PARTNERS

Designed by architect Nic Bochsler, this two-storey house provides a striking contrast to many of the neighbouring homes. Finished with black tiles, the home is beautifully framed by birch trees and creepers. "The owners come from India. They loved natural finishes, such as stone", says Bochsler. His clients also have an affinity with black – they drive black cars and love collecting black objects. ■ While Bochsler is masterful in using black, it's rare that he designs an all-black house, with black used to complement his often white-rendered homes. However, keen for an all-black house, with a brief calling for low-maintenance, Bochsler suggested tiles for the exterior. "You can simply wash the walls down with a hose. It's considerably less work than if the walls are rendered and painted black", he says. ■ Bochsler used a black pebble-rendered finish for the canopies. And to allow the house to enjoy verdant outlooks, he also included black steel awnings in the design. These awnings, which extend to the roof, allow for creepers. These awnings also create privacy, as well as reducing the effect of the afternoon sunlight. ■ In contrast to the all-black exterior, the interior of the house is a striking combination of black and white. The indoor swimming pool, for example, is fully lined with black tiles. This accentuates the white marble surrounding the pool. A soaring glass wall adjacent to the pool also includes black steel-framed windows. And to strengthen the connection with the outdoors, Bochsler used the same black tiles on the exterior of the double-height wall that frames the indoor pool. ■ Black also appears in the kitchen, which features black Imperite benches and joinery. These lacquered finishes become more animated against the light. And although there are white tiles on the kitchen floor, many of the living spaces are finished with black granite floors. ■ This highly graphic interior also allows for a mixture of furnishings, from antiques through to contemporary. "I wanted to create a fairly neutral palette to allow the owners to put their own stamp on their home", adds Bochsler. ■ PHOTOGRAPHY: NEIL LORIMER

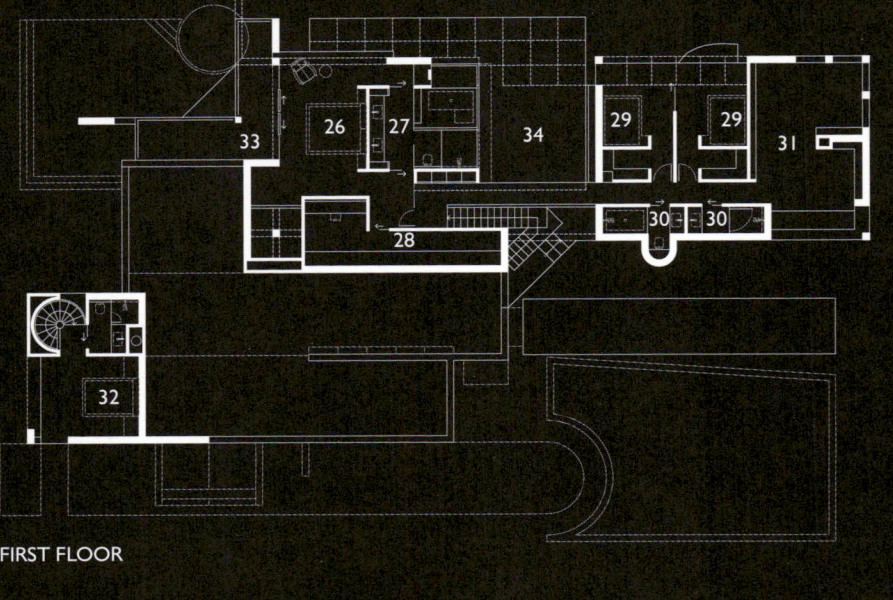

FIRST FLOOR

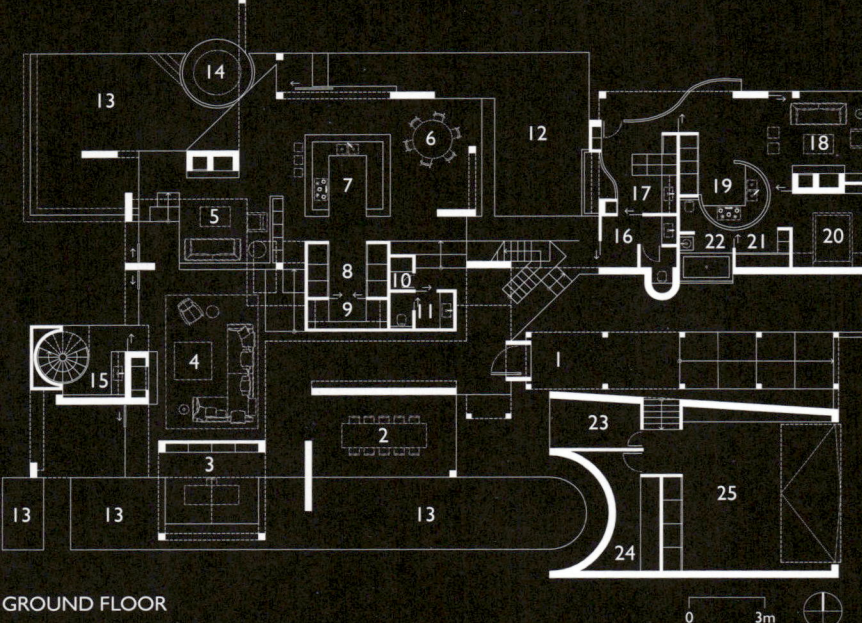

GROUND FLOOR

1	Entry	18	Guest living room
2	Dining	19	Guest kitchenette
3	Study	20	Guest bedroom
4	Living	21	Guest walk-in wardrobe
5	Family	22	Guest ensuite
6	Breakfast	23	Plant
7	Kitchen	24	Store
8	Butler	25	Garage
9	Pantry	26	Master bedroom
10	Cloakroom	27	Master ensuite
11	Powder room	28	Master walk-in wardrobe
12	Internal pool	29	Bedroom
13	Outdoor pool	30	Bathroom
14	Spa	31	Play room
15	Bar	32	Guest bedroom
16	Changing room	33	Balcony
17	Laundry	34	Void

Back to

ROOM 11

BLACK

This house in Kingston, Hobart, is on the last bush block in the street and one of the few remaining in the suburb. A slope of 25 degrees may have been one reason the site remained vacant for so long. With panoramic views from Mount Wellington to Kingston beach, the Tasmanian property was calling out for something quite special. "Our clients wanted a house that was calm and tranquil, a place to retreat at the end of each day", says designer Aaron Roberts, who worked closely with founding member of Room 11, Thomas Bailey. ■ The Kingston house, clad in plywood and stained black, floats on a suspended concrete slab supported by steel columns. On the ground floor of the 240-square-metre home are two guest bedrooms and a bathroom. And on the first floor, also at the point of entry, are the living areas, a kitchen, studio, main bedroom, ensuite and dressing area. Voids run between the two levels. The main void provides space for three ornamental pear trees, while the second void, visible only from the main bedroom, features a Japanese maple. "We wanted to create a seasonal clock, with deciduous trees colouring the internal areas of the home as the seasons change", says Roberts, who collaborated with his colleagues, designers Nathan Crump and James Wilson. ■ Given the pristine site, Room 11 was keen to design a house that receded into the landscape, rather than dominate it. "Our initial ideas came from sitting on this rock shelf. We didn't want to eliminate any views, from the mountains to the beach", says Roberts. Views from the rock shelf and entry point to the mountain were maintained by glass walls either side of the living area, facing the internal void and the distant mountain beyond. ■ With 180-degree views through floor-to-ceiling glass windows, the house can be likened to a floating platform. The living room, for instance, is elevated 3.5 metres above the ground and there's a bridge-like living area linking the main bedroom to the kitchen. ■ While the dark exterior recedes into the Australian bush, there are pockets of 'intensity' within the house. White glossy joinery illuminates the darkened shell, and the bathroom, adjacent to the main bedroom, is lined with flamboyant baroque patterned tiles. The downstairs bathroom is also bold, with large gloss-red tiles adorning the walls. "It's about the site. Even when you're looking in the bathroom mirror, you can see the reflection of the trees", adds Roberts. ■ PHOTOGRAPHY: JASMIN LATONA

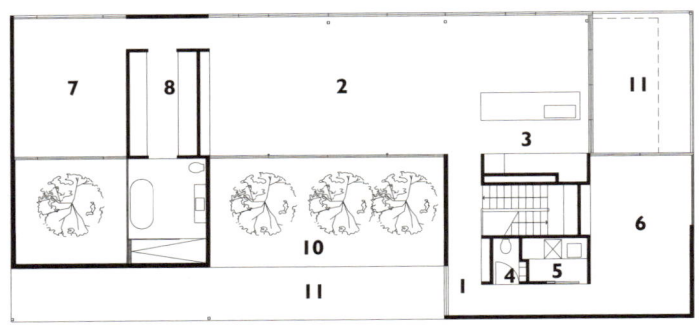

UPPER LEVEL

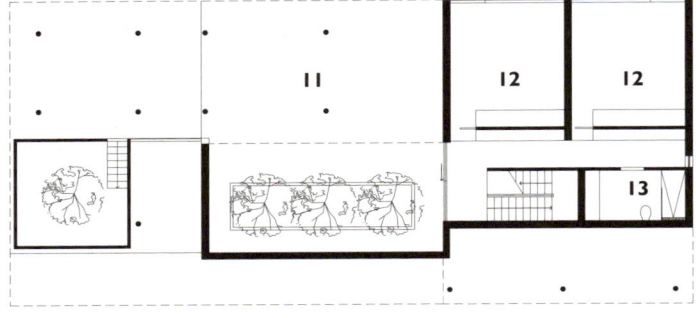

LOWER LEVEL

1 Entry
2 Living/dining
3 Kitchen
4 Powder room
5 Laundry
6 Studio
7 Master bedroom
8 Walk-in wardrobe
9 Ensuite
10 Void
11 Deck
12 Bedroom
13 Bathroom

SHEER

CASEY BROWN ARCHITECTURE

Designed by Casey Brown Architecture, this house, overlooking Sydney's Pittwater, can be accessed only by boat. When the house was being constructed, a boat, as well as a helicopter, was needed to transport materials. "It's an extremely steep site (approximately 60 degrees). It was a challenge building this house", says architect Rob Brown, one of the directors of the practice. ■ This house, separated into two pavilions, borders a national park. "Our clients were keen for a pavilion-style home. But they also appreciated the difficulty of building anything too monumental in terms of construction", says Brown. ■ The pavilion on the higher part of the site consists of the main bedroom and bathroom. There's also a laundry below. To reach the pavilion, there's a short steep climb or alternatively an inclinator. The main pavilion, occupying the lower portion of the site, includes the kitchen and living areas, with the lounge enjoying a double-height volume. Below the main pavilion are two guest bedrooms, a bathroom and cellar. ■ As the site is precarious, the architects used black steel, as well as copper for roofs and walls. The window- and doorframes are also black steel. Contrasting the black steel is a sandstone base that anchors the home. "We had to excavate into the hilltop and thought it was appropriate to express the terrain", says Brown. ■ While the sandstone creates an earthy base, the black steel provides sharp edges when placed against blue skies. "The black steel we used has small profiles. It allows for fine, razor-sharp edges", says Brown. Using black also related to the site, surrounded by a national park. "The house is part of the landscape. It recedes rather than screaming for attention", adds Brown. ■ PHOTOGRAPHY: ANTHONY BROWELL AND PATRICK BINGHAM-HALL

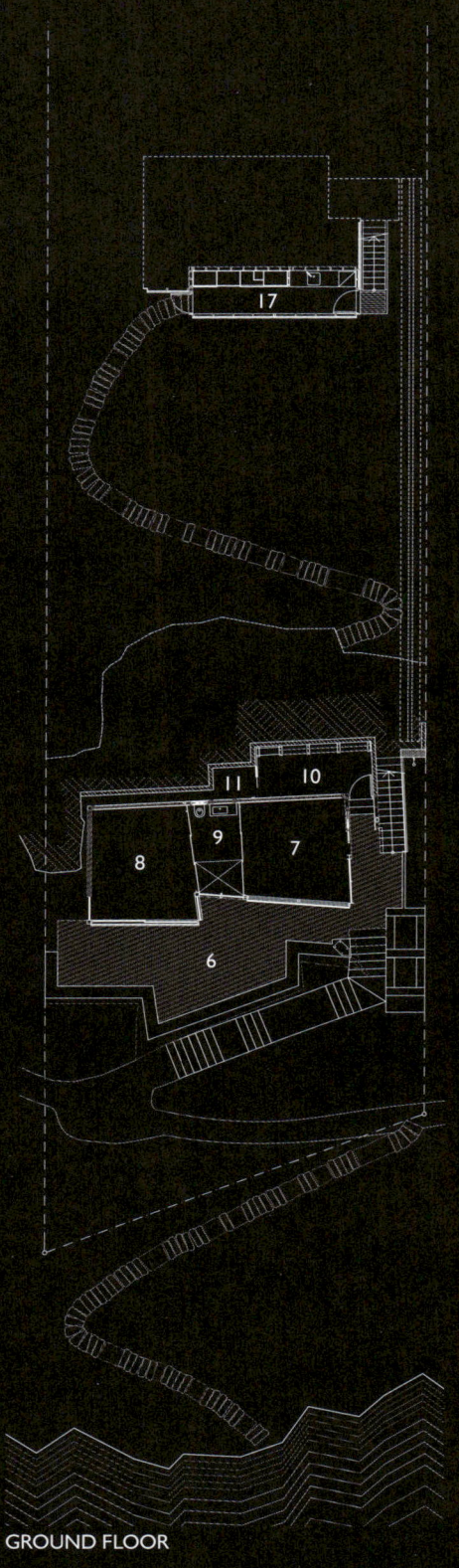
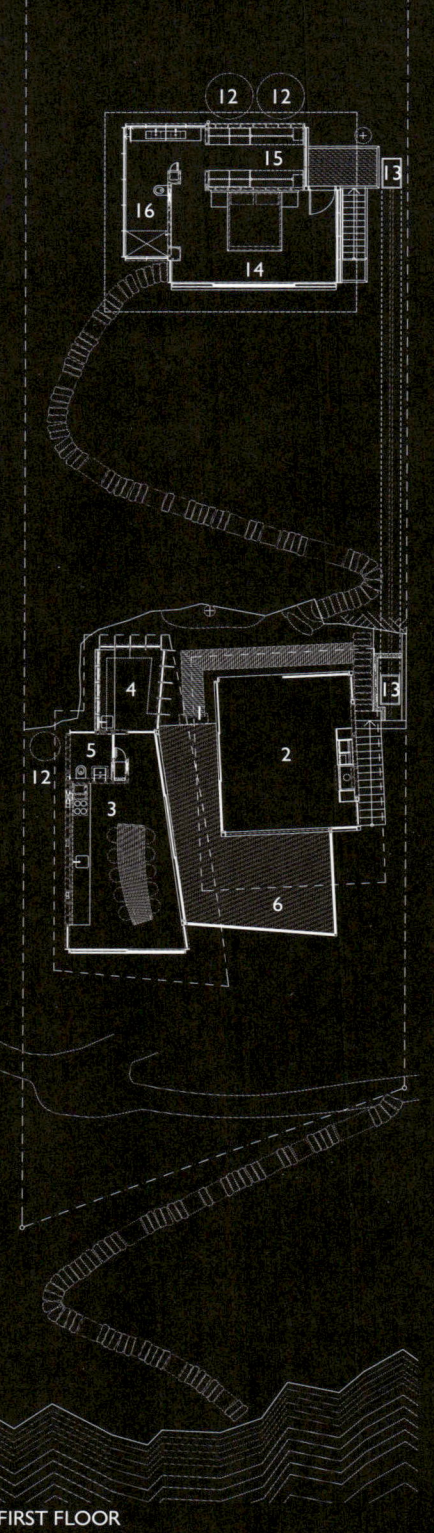

GROUND FLOOR

FIRST FLOOR

1	Entry	10	Cellar
2	Living	11	Plant room
3	Kitchen/dining	12	Water tank
4	Pantry	13	Inclinator
5	Powder room	14	Master bedroom
6	Deck	15	Walk-in wardrobe
7	Study	16	Ensuite
8	Guest bedroom	17	Laundry
9	Bathroom		

RAMMED

WOOD / MARSH ARCHITECTURE

his home on Victoria's Mornington Peninsula is monumental in appearance. Two large rammed earth walls bisect a series of black stained timber forms, each one enclosing rooms within the home. "With many buildings built during the 18th and 19th centuries there are a series of rooms connected by a breezeway such as a verandah", says architect Rodger Wood, co-director of Wood / Marsh. "That breezeway is often used as a means of navigating your way through a place", he adds. ■ At the point of entry of this home, there's a timber-clad box that appears to 'stand proud' of one of the rammed earth walls. This is the garage, complete with black stained timber door. Past the front door, Wood / Marsh's design cleverly unfolds, with the rammed earth walls and undulating ceiling of the corridor (varying in height from 2.7 metres to 5 metres) directing the eye to either large open-plan spaces or dramatic vistas overlooking Bass Strait. "One of the challenges with the site was that the main views of the ocean correlated to the strongest winds. While the house turns its back on the wind, it still captures the views", says Wood. ■ While the initial brief for this house didn't include the colour black, it did stipulate a need for zoning both parents' and children's areas, together with guest accommodation. At the front of the house are the children's bedrooms and bathrooms, as well as a bedroom for guests. Bisecting the plan of the house is a lap pool, together with a sheltered outdoor area for outdoor dining. The swimming pool is lined with black tiles and there are black stained timber beams on the terrace diffusing the light. At the other end of the house, past the living areas, and slightly elevated is the main bedroom wing. ■ Wood / Marsh included black steel fireplaces in their design, one of which appears on the terrace to allow for outdoor dining through the cooler months of the year. And some of the walls inside the house are painted black. "Black is a perfect backdrop for art. It intensifies the colour of a painting", says Wood. "It's also an ideal colour against natural materials, such as rammed earth", he adds. ■ PHOTOGRAPHY

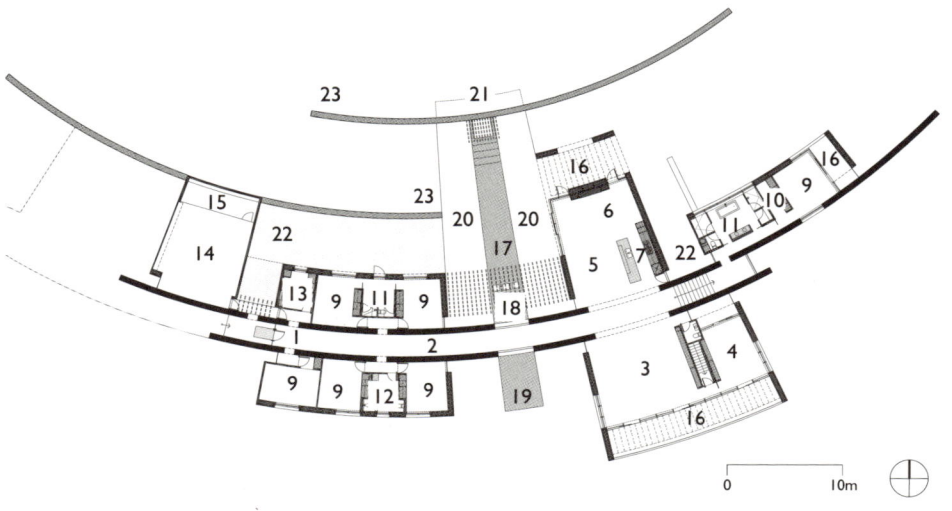

FLOOR PLAN

1	Entry	13	Laundry
2	Corridor	14	Garage
3	Living	15	Store
4	Study	16	Terrace
5	Dining	17	Pool
6	Lounge	18	Spa
7	Kitchen	19	Pond
8	Powder room	20	Pool terrace
9	Bedroom	21	Pool equipment
10	Walk-in wardrobe	22	Courtyard
11	Bathroom	23	Garden wall
12	Ensuite		

Top

b.e ARCHITECTURE

When Broderick Ely, design director for b.e architecture, found this house, he knew he could rework it into a contemporary home for his family. While the house, built in the early 20th century, was totally run down, it had great bones, as well as a great aspect over a large garden. "The house has been completely reworked, both in terms of spaces and detailing", says Ely. ■ The front living room, for example, was transformed into a main bedroom, with the adjacent bedroom becoming a bathroom and walk-in dressing area. One of the other bedrooms was converted into a music room; and replacing the tired kitchen and meals area is a new open-plan wing. Framed with white bricks that have been heavily mortared, the new wing appears sharp and crisp. "I removed most of the original detailing. There were a couple of oddly placed corners that would have made the renovation appear neither contemporary nor period", says Ely. ■ While the new wing is white, entry to the house is via large black painted timber gates. Ely also designed a side entry, complete with a mud room for his children to leave their school bags and shoes. Clad in timber and painted black, there's an appropriate juxtaposition between the home's original red bricks and this black point of arrival. ■ The second level of this house comprises two bedrooms and a bathroom, together with a study nook. And like the side entrance, this floor is entirely black. Made from zincalume, the profile is deliberately random. "This profile was customised for me. I find that when something is too regular, your eye tends to skirt over it. This profile tends to be noticed", says Ely, who likens the first floor to a smart top hat. ■ In contrast to the black exterior, the interior of this home is almost all white, exceptions being steel balustrades on the staircase, together with some customised wrought-iron light fittings. The new fireplace in the music room is also black. The black exterior makes the interior appear more dramatic. It's that contrast, like the contrast between the original part of the house and the new top hat that makes this design so striking. ■ PHOTOGRAPHY: PETER CLARKE

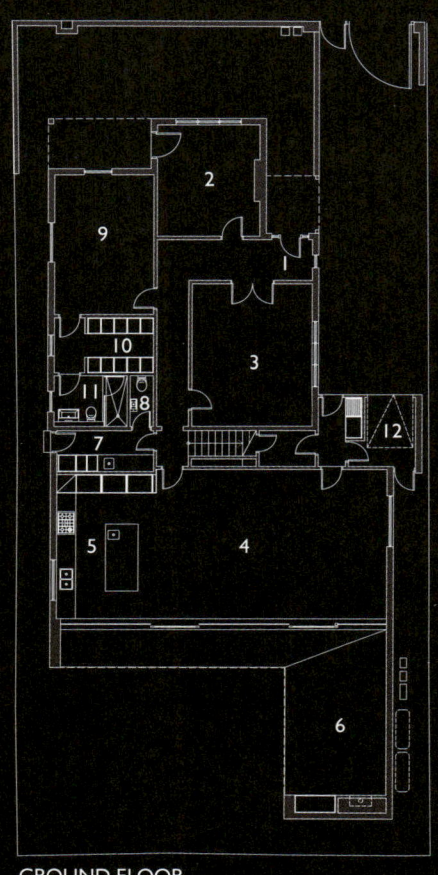

GROUND FLOOR

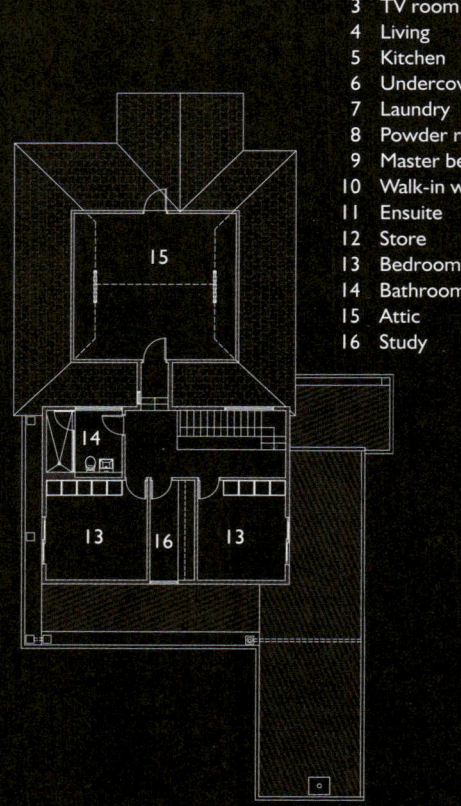

FIRST FLOOR

1 Entry
2 Music room
3 TV room
4 Living
5 Kitchen
6 Undercover dining
7 Laundry
8 Powder room
9 Master bedroom
10 Walk-in wardrobe
11 Ensuite
12 Store
13 Bedroom
14 Bathroom
15 Attic
16 Study

Index of Architects

1+2 Architecture 116, 176
www.1plus2architecture.com

Andres Remy Arquitectos 38
www.andresremy.com

Andrew Simpson Architects 11, 80, 98
www.asimpson.com.au

b.e architecture 86, 218
www.bearchitecture.com

Bellemo & Cat 56
www.bellemocat.com.au

Bochsler + Partners 194
www.bochsler.com

Bower Architecture 92
www.bowerarchitecture.com.au

Case Ornsby 110
www.caseornsby.com.au

Casey Brown Architecture 206
www.caseybrown.com.au

Chenchow Little Architects 18, 32
www.chenchowlittle.com

Choi Ropiha Fighera 16, 20
www.chrofi.com

David Edelman Architects 158
www.dearchitects.com

dKO Architecture 188
www.dko.com.au

Fabre/deMarien 68
www.fabredemarien.com

Ian Moore Architects 12, 26
www.ianmoorearchitects.com

Inarc Architects 182
www.inarc.com.au

Intermode 62
www.intermode.com.au

Jason Bailey Architecture + Design Management 128
www.jasonbailey.co.nz

John Wardle Architects 152
www.johnwardlearchitects.com.au

Kennedy Nolan Architects 140
www.kennedynolan.com.au

Marc Dixon Architect 50
www.marcdixon.com

Matter 122
www.matter.co.nz

Muir Mendes 44
www.muirmendes.com

Nixon Tulloch Fortey Architecture 13, 14, 15
www.ntfarchitecture.com.au

Nord Architecture 134
www.nordarchitecture.com

Room 11 200
www.room11.com.au

Stevens Lawson Architects 104
www.stevenslawson.co.nz

Strachan Group Architects 17, 164
www.sgaltd.co.nz

studiofour 10
www.studiofour.com

Terroir 74
www.terroir.com.au

Tobin Smith Architect 110
www.tobinsmitharchitect.com

Wood / Marsh Architecture 212
www.woodmarsh.com.au

XSite Architects 146
www.xsite.net.nz

Zoeller Design 19, 170
joshua.zoeller@gmail.com

Every effort has been made to trace the original source of copyright material contained in this book. The publishers would be pleased to hear from copyright holders to rectify any errors or omissions.

The information and illustrations in this publication have been prepared and supplied by the contributors. While all reasonable efforts have been made to ensure accuracy, the publishers do not, under any circumstances, accept responsibility for errors, omissions and representations, express or implied.